Godliness and Contentment
Studies in the Pastoral Epistles

Marcus L. Loane

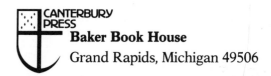

CANTERBURY
PRESS
Baker Book House
Grand Rapids, Michigan 49506

Copyright 1982 by
Baker Book House Company

ISBN: 0-8010-5619-5

Printed in the United States of America

This book is inscribed
in token of friendship
for the Right Reverend
John Robert Reid
and his wife
Alison

Contents

This book is a series of studies in the three Pauline Letters known as the pastoral epistles. The text of the Revised Version (1881) has been quoted throughout, unless another translation has been indicated. It is assumed that the author of the pastoral epistles was Paul in the last phase of his career. The letters are treated in the order in which they must have been written; internal evidence is a reasonable guide in chronology. It is further assumed that the epistles belong to a later stage in Paul's life than the imprisonment in Rome described by Luke in the Book of Acts. That book came to an end on a note of calm and confidence: "And he abode two whole years in his own hired dwelling, and received all that went in unto him, preaching the kingdom of God and teaching the things concerning the Lord Jesus Christ with all boldness, none forbidding him" (Acts 28:30–31). But the circumstances of Paul's imprisonment described in his final letter to Timothy were in total contrast with the optimism of that earlier situation. It seems certain that that imprisonment ended with Paul's discharge; he was released from formal restraint and restored to freedom. Whether or not he had fulfilled his plan to visit Spain we cannot tell (Rom. 15:24), but he certainly visited old scenes on each side of the Aegean Sea. He strengthened and confirmed his converts in the faith; he made arrangements for the leadership and discipline of the churches; he reached out to new points for witness and evangelism; he left the most experienced men in the most strategic areas. He wrote to Timothy in Ephesus and Titus in Crete with detailed and varied instructions. Then perhaps through delators or informers Paul was placed under arrest apparently on a charge of treason. He was transferred to Rome whence he wrote his final letter to Timothy under the shadow of imminent martyrdom.

The first letter began with a declaration of Paul's authority in order to mark the authority of all that would follow:[1] "Paul, an apostle of Christ Jesus according to the commandment of God our Saviour, and Christ Jesus our hope; unto Timothy, my true child in faith: Grace, mercy, peace from God the Father and Christ Jesus our Lord" (1:1–2). God our Saviour is identical with God the Father, while the thrice-repeated names Christ Jesus, in that order, mark the Messianic identity of Him who is both our hope and our Lord. Paul launched himself at once into angry seas of controversy in order to counsel the man who had to bear the brunt of the trouble. Paul had exhorted Timothy to remain at Ephesus while he undertook a journey into Macedonia. There were certain men whom Timothy was to warn not to teach a different doctrine nor to waste time on such irrelevant issues as fables and endless genealogies. Indeed Paul's words were so rapid that the grammar broke down and he left the sentence without an end. His intention is clarified in the Revised Version by the insertion of the words in italics: *"so do I now"* (1:4). It is clear that there was a firm standard of truth; but heresy and fantasy had great appeal. "But," wrote Paul, "the end of the charge is love out of a pure heart and a good conscience and faith unfeigned" (1:5). Paul's deep sense of alarm sprang from the fact that some had swerved so as to miss the mark and turned aside so as to drift off course.[2] Some teachers were eager to teach the law, but they had scant understanding of the gospel. "They understand neither what they say," Paul wrote, "nor whereof they confidently affirm" (1:7). That indictment was terrible; their ignorance was appalling.

---

1. Donald Guthrie, *The Pastoral Epistles, An Introduction and Commentary*, p. 55.
2. Ibid., p. 60.

But what was the role of the law? Its main purpose was to restrain those who would do evil: "But," wrote Paul, "we know that the law is good, if a man use it lawfully" (1:8). The word *lawfully* (II Tim. 2:5) is the key to this verse. Paul was strenuously opposed to the empty-headed speculation of the self-styled teachers to whom he had referred (1:7), but he never sought to deny the true nobility of law in the purpose of God. This was made clear as he went on to say "that law is not made for a righteous man, but for the lawless and unruly, for the ungodly and sinners, for the unholy and profane" (1:9). Such men had made themselves guilty of an offense against the God who gave the law. The lawless were those who lived as though there were no law; the unruly were those who had thrown off every form of discipline; the ungodly were those who had lost all reverence for God; the sinners were those who had defied God as open rebels; the unholy were those for whom nothing was sacred; the profane were those who would barter spiritual birthrights for a mess of pottage. The list runs on to touch on the most violent or horrific of crimes against mankind; the kind of crime, that is, with which human lawcourts can deal. It paints in the darkest colors a most somber picture of the society in the Levant where Paul had been at work. The list is rounded off with a last comprehensive statement: "and if there be any other thing contrary to the sound doctrine" (1:10). This may seem a surprising conclusion to the terrible catalogue of law-breakers, but it formed the preface to Paul's final statement in this section about "the gospel of the glory of the blessed God, which was committed to my trust" (1:11). Those words placed Paul firmly on the home ground of a profound experience in his own soul and led to a splendid fragment of autobiography. So let us now read on.

*"Faithful is the saying, and worthy of all
acceptation, that Christ Jesus came into the
world to save sinners; of whom I am chief."*

I Timothy 1:15

Paul had rounded off a stringent warning with an appeal
to "the gospel of the glory of the blessed God which was
committed to my trust" (1:11). He caught fire at the thought of
the glory of God, "so radiantly reflected in the gospel" with
which he had been put in trust.[1] It set alight a train of thought
which provides a luminous insight into his constant sense of
wonder at the grace of God: "I thank him that enabled me,
even Christ Jesus our Lord, for that he counted me faithful,
appointing me to his service" (1:12). Paul's heart never ceased
to sing with praise for Him who had made Paul able (Phil.
4:13), and he spoke of Him by name and title with an impressive emphasis: the Christ, even Jesus, who is our Lord. That
phrase was a complete and succinct condensation of Paul's
theology: Jesus is the unique person in whom messianic
dignity and universal dominion were fulfilled. All that the
Jews looked for as the hope of Israel, and all that the gentiles
thought of as the Lord of the world, was found in Him. It was
this same Jesus who is both Lord and Christ who had chosen
Paul as one who was trustworthy for His service. And the
exceeding grace which underlay such a choice was evident
in that Paul had been "a blasphemer, and a persecutor, and

1. E. K. Simpson, *The Pastoral Epistles*, p. 32.

injurious" (1:13). He could never forget the fact that he had tried to stamp out the name of Jesus; he could never excuse the fact that he had tried to destroy the church of God. Paul had acted in the spirit of violence and arrogance; and yet he had "obtained mercy" (1:13). The grace of God reached out toward Paul in infinite tenderness because he was blinded by ignorance and unbelief, and that grace was channeled to him "in Christ Jesus" (1:14).

All that Paul had written so far served no higher purpose than to form the preface for his next words, and so weighty were those words that they were ushered in by their own distinctive formula: "Faithful is the saying, and worthy of all acceptation" (1:15). The word *faithful* occurs seventeen times in the pastoral epistles, and it is linked with a particular saying five times (I Tim. 3:1; 4:9; II Tim. 2:11; Titus 3:8). In three verses, the formula is laconic: "Faithful is the saying." In two others, it is strengthened by additional words: "and worthy of all acceptation" (I Tim. 1:15; 4:9). But whether laconic or extended in form, these five faithful sayings have a rhythmical quality which would make them the more easily remembered. They were current watchwords in the churches, so phrased that they lent themselves for use in chant or song. Paul exhorted the churches of Ephesus and Colossae to cultivate this spirit: they were to cheer and encourage one another with psalms and hymns and songs, "singing and making melody with your heart to the Lord; giving thanks always for all things in the name of our Lord Jesus Christ" (Eph. 5:19–20). When Pliny the younger was proconsul of the Roman province of Bithynia, he consulted the Emperor Trajan as to how he should deal with those who were professing Christians. Pliny had already made some inquiries; the Christians seemed harmless enough. He found that they met early in the morning to sing "a hymn of praise to Christ as God." Here was unwitting evidence from a pagan writer that Jesus was worshiped as God, and that hymns of praise were part of that worship.

This sure word was one on which they could depend as altogether reliable and which deserved to be received by all. What was this word? It was "that Christ Jesus came into the world to save sinners." These words are a perfect definition of the gospel. It would be hard to frame a sentence in the English language so simple, so lucid, so concise, which more perfectly represents that great good news. Christ came down from heaven into the world, out of eternity into time; He was clothed with human nature, became a babe in arms; He was the true Emmanuel, the God who is with us; and He came with one grand object in view: He came to save sinners. This verse directs our thoughts to the two great focal points of the whole gospel; it draws a straight line from the manger at Bethlehem to the cross on Calvary. He came, by that mighty act of incarnation; He came to save, by that terrible atonement. He came into the world: "For God so loved the world that He gave His only begotten Son" (John 3:16). He came to save sinners: for "God commendeth his own love toward us, in that, while we were yet sinners, Christ died for us" (Rom. 5:8). One may try to look from every angle, but this verse always tells the same story. He came into the world. Why? Was it only to share our trials or to bear our sorrows? No, it was to save sinners. He came to save sinners. How? Was it as a helpless babe or as a sinless man? No, it was by His cross and passion. He was made flesh when He was born of the Virgin Mary at His coming into the world (John 1:14); He was made sin when He bowed His head and died in the place of sinners (II Cor. 5:21). It is Jesus Christ, incarnate and crucified, who is man's only Savior.

This great declaration was reinforced by a moving personal reference: "Of whom I am chief" (I Tim. 1:15). Paul turned from Christ as the only Savior to that man whom he saw as the foremost among sinners. Paul could hardly speak of himself at all except through the use of superlatives. If he were to look in the direction of those who were saints, he was "the least" (I Cor. 15:9); nay more, "less than the least" (Eph.

3:8). If he were to look in the direction of those who were sinners, he was the chief, perhaps even the worst (NIV). This was not the language of formal self-abasement, but the cry of unaffected humility. Paul saw himself as the chief of sinners, the worst of men, because his hands had once been red with the blood of the saints. He had thrown men into prison and had pursued them to the point of death (Acts 26:10). And now he was haunted by the specter of his early career of violence and blasphemy. He could not forgive himself nor dissolve the shadows of the wrong he had done. All the cumulative guilt of frenzied persecution crystallized in a final cry of unhealed agony: "And when the blood of thy martyr Stephen was shed, I also was standing by and consenting unto his death" (Acts 22:20, AV). Paul could see no mercy for a man like himself should he be left to his just desert. But the grace of God met him in his darkest hour and in his utmost distress. Paul cast his soul at last on the mercies of God, and those mercies more than matched his need. And if there were mercy for him, who is there for whom the Lord may not have mercy? It was therefore Paul's own experience of that astonishing mercy which led him to declare that what he had written was "a faithful saying"; he would commend it as "worthy of all acceptation."

This great text has had a long and notable history. It is not too much to say that it was the key to the English Reformation and the makers of its theology. The story begins with Thomas Bilney, a shy and gentle student of law at Trinity Hall in Cambridge. He had long felt in a vague and indefinite way the emptiness of the religion in which he had been born and bred. His soul was sick and he longed for peace, but could find it nowhere. He knelt at the feet of unlearned confessors and itemized all his sins; they could only prescribe various penances, such as fasts and vigils, payment for masses, purchase of pardons. But such things were merely broken cisterns that mocked his thirst. At last he heard of the Novum Testamentum which was published by Erasmus in March

1519. This was the second edition of the New Testament in Greek which had first been published as the Novum Instrumentum in March 1516. Little Bilney, as he was called, bought a copy as much for the beauty of the Latin translation by Erasmus as for its contents. But the hand of God was on him, and the very first time he sat down to read it, he chanced on the words of this text: "It is a true saying and worthy of all men to be embraced, that Christ Jesus came into the world to save sinners; of whom I am the chief." Each word stood out as it were in letters of light, and that light shone into his heart. "O most sweet and comfortable sentence to my soul!" he exclaimed. Bilney did not break from the church, even though he saw her sins with clear-eyed reality; nor did he grasp the whole scheme of Reformation theology, even though he felt its power with increased understanding. But Bilney was the first Cambridge scholar to take his stand for the Reformation, for he had found peace with God through faith in Christ as the only Savior.[2]

Little Bilney soon became the moving spirit among a group of men who met in the White Horse Inn for the study of the New Testament. "So oft as I was in their company," wrote Thomas Becon, "methought I was . . . in the new glorious Jerusalem."[3] Bilney had an almost naive belief that others would respond to the gospel as he had done if only they heard it. He told the story of his experience both to Hugh Latimer and to Cuthbert Tunstall. The one believed, while the other did not respond. Bilney's text and testimony became widely known in Cambridge circles, and one of those who heard it was Thomas Cranmer while he was still a fellow of Jesus College. Cranmer's mind was open to the teaching of the Scriptures; he read widely and slowly moved toward the light. Cranmer's conversion was finally evident when he published the first *Book of Common Prayer* in 1549.

2. Marcus L. Loane, *Masters of the English Reformation*, pp. 5–8.
3. Thomas Becon, *The Catechism with Other Pieces*, (Parker Society), p. 426.

He embedded in the service of the Holy Communion four New Testament quotations which he introduced as "comfortable words." Two of these were sayings chosen from the gospel records. One was a verse from the First Epistle of Saint John; the other was taken from one of the Pauline letters. If the task had fallen to a modern liturgiologist to make that choice, he might have felt overwhelmed; how would he choose just one "comfortable word" from so rich a store? Cranmer had no hesitation, he knew the one verse which had a unique place in the hearts of the English Reformers. "Hear what St. Paul saith," he wrote. "This is a true saying, and worthy of all men to be received, that Christ Jesus came into the world to save sinners." Little Bilney died at the stake in the Lollards' Pit at Norwich in 1531; Cranmer was burned to death outside the walls of an Oxford College in 1556. But they had heard "what St. Paul saith," and that text had poured its comfort into their hearts and made them bright with the hope of glory.

"Howbeit for this cause I obtained mercy, that in me as chief might Jesus Christ shew forth all his longsuffering, for an ensample of them which should hereafter believe on him unto eternal life."

I Timothy 1:16

Paul was overwhelmed by "the magnitude of God's grace";[1] he could never refer to it in his own case without being moved to expand the theme. His great encounter on the road to Damascus was an indelible experience; thirty years later he spoke of it with as much freshness as if it had happened only a month or two before. Those who heard him might be hostile or indifferent, casual or cynical, interested or sympathetic; but whatever their attitude, it could not quench the flame of that testimony which glowed like a fire in his heart. Paul had to tell what God had done for him because it was so great an act of grace; he saw himself as a living illustration of God's mercy toward the greatest of sinners. It was one thing to say that the gospel is good news for bad men; it was far more to know that that was why it was good news for him. That was enough to prove that Paul's conversion was an example of what God is willing to do for all who cast themselves on His mercy. Therefore the line of thought in this passage moved quite naturally from Christ Jesus as the mighty Savior to Paul himself as the chief of

1. Guthrie, *Pastoral Epistles*, p. 65.

sinners. Then he took up the word *chief* or *foremost* in order to expound what he knew to be God's purpose in that act of mercy: "Howbeit for this cause I obtained mercy, that in me as chief might Jesus Christ shew forth all his longsuffering, for an ensample of them which should hereafter believe on him unto eternal life" (1:16). The word *chief* or *foremost* is the main link between the two verses; it marks the strong personal emphasis in the ongoing argument. But the role of Jesus Christ is equally prominent except that the order of His names is reversed. Jesus was His human name, and it stands here before the more formal messianic title of Christ. This was only a small change, but in this context, it was very fitting, for He was called Jesus because He came to save men from their sins (Matt. 1:21).

This verse reiterates Paul's moving testimony to the grace and mercy of God so that he could relate what had happened in his case to God's loving concern for all who will believe: "Howbeit for this cause I obtained mercy, that in me as chief might Jesus Christ shew forth all his longsuffering." But this sentence reaches back to an earlier utterance and its first words are a verbatim quotation of words in that statement: "I was before a blasphemer, and a persecutor, and injurious: howbeit I obtained mercy, because I did it ignorantly in unbelief" (1:13). The life he had led as Saul of Tarsus must have put him at an immense distance from the mercy of God, and yet, in spite of this, mercy was bestowed on Paul when his implacable hostility was at its height. If any man ever needed to hear the most gracious words of promise in the Old Testament, it was surely Saul of Tarsus: "Though your sins be as scarlet, they shall be as white as snow; though they be red like crimson, they shall be as wool" (Isa. 1:18). Sin is a thing of time, but mercy is everlasting; there was mercy for him even when he could not see mercy for himself. But the mercy of God in Paul's case was not without special reason. It was "for this cause;" it had in view its own special purpose. It was not for Saul's sake alone; it was for the sake of the far wider circle of humanity in generations to come. Paul saw himself as the foremost among sinners; therefore it was fitting that in him *first* (AV) the Lord Jesus should manifest His longsuffering. It was Paul's experience of that divine longsuffering that had lent such pathos to his appeal on an earlier occasion: "Despisest thou the riches of his goodness and forbearance and longsuffering, not knowing that the goodness of God leadeth thee to repentance?" (Rom. 2:4).

The march of thought led to a yet larger declaration of God's gracious purpose in His choice of Saul of Tarsus: it was "for an ensample of them which should hereafter believe on him unto eternal life" (1:16). Paul could never escape for long from his innermost conviction that the grace of God was seen in its most amazing exercise in his case; this was why he saw his conversion as an example of God's gracious design for all who will only believe. The word *example* (RSV) made its appearance with a different translation in a later passage: "Hold the pattern of sound words which thou hast heard from me" (II Tim. 1:13). E. K. Simpson observes that the Greek term denotes a word-picture, and goes on to argue that this suits the context of Paul's declaration.[2] What God did for Paul was a pattern of what God is able to do in the case of others. It was not as though Paul made a choice for God; God chose Paul in spite of all his sin and provocation. And if mercy laid its hand on him, there is no one who may not come under the same divine arrest. That was why he dared to say that his own dramatic conversion would serve as a compelling example for all who in ages to come were to believe on Him. They would not be required to do, but only to believe; not to obey, but to respond with trust. The use of the particular preposition with the dative case after the word *believe* was rare in Paul's letters, but he employed it twice in a quotation from the Old Testament: "He that believeth on

2. Simpson, *Pastoral Epistles*, p. 36.

19

Him shall not be put to shame" (Rom. 9:33; 10:11). The faith that leads to eternal life must be rooted in Him, that is, in Christ Jesus who came to save sinners.

Is such a thing as a pattern experience of the grace and mercy of God a valid and reliable signpost for men today? Latimer's conversion in the light of Bilney's experience answers in the affirmative with the boldest Amen. Hugh Latimer, fellow of Clare Hall in Cambridge, won universal admiration for rugged honesty and homely eloquence. But he was a devout son of the church who was strongly opposed to the Reformation. Bilney saw that Latimer was caught in the same toils which had been a snare to him, and Bilney's heart went out to Latimer with a great love and longing for his deliverance. He was only Little Bilney and would never do any great service for God; but let him win the soul of that one man and what great things would Latimer do in His name? Bilney seized his chance when he found Latimer in his study. Bilney begged Latimer for the love of God to hear his confession. There was Bilney with his pale face and his wasted features and his perfect sincerity, asking Latimer to shrive his soul; what could it all mean? Latimer did not understand, but he watched and listened as Bilney fell on his knees and told all that was in his heart. Latimer heard Bilney's story of conflict and anguish as he had gone about seeking health and healing for his sick soul. Latimer heard how Bilney had been bruised and broken at the hands of ignorant physicians until at last he was healed as he read the Novum Testamentum. And would he not draw that Book out of his pocket and let it fall open at the words he had so often read? "It is a true saying and worthy of all men to be embraced, that Christ Jesus came into the world to save sinners." Latimer was taken by storm. Bilney's experience was the pattern for a decisive conversion, for it was to Latimer rather than to Bilney that the Word of God came in absolution that day.[3]

3. Loane, *Masters of the English Reformation*, pp. 11–12.

Paul could never lose his sense of wonder at God's long-suffering toward a rebel such as he had been, and he magnified God's act of grace in his conversion as a pattern of what God is willing to do for all who will believe. Another example of God's infinite forbearance may be found in the case of John Newton, the seafarer and slave trader of the mid-eighteenth century. Newton had been seized by a naval press gang and had tried to desert, but was caught, stripped, and flogged. He was transferred to a ship for the West Indies and then to a slave merchant on the coast of West Africa. Newton sank so low in destitution and degradation that he lost all hope. But he was rescued by a friendly captain on a passing vessel and at last, in January 1748, the sails were set for home. But the ship ran into so fierce a storm that he had to be lashed to the pumps from three in the morning until midday. Worn out with cold and hard labor, he was struck with a thought that had not crossed his mind for years. If all their pains did not avail, let the Lord have mercy on them; but what mercy, he began to wonder, could there be for a man like him? "I thought . . . there never was nor could be such a sinner as myself; and then . . . I concluded . . . that my sins were too great to be forgiven."[4] It was only a step, but that step led him at length to a firm trust in the Lord Jesus. Newton left the sea and was ordained; his ministry was divided between Olney and London; and his hymns and letters made him one of the best-known clergy in England. William Jay of Bath came to see Newton on his deathbed in 1807. Newton's mind and mouth were almost beyond effort, but one priceless saying fell from his lips. "My memory is nearly gone," he whispered, "but I remember two things, that I am a great sinner and that Christ is a great Saviour."[5]

The thought structure in this passage is marked by a

4. Marcus L. Loane, *Oxford and the Evangelical Succession*, p. 90.
5. Ibid., p. 130.

double movement: it moves from the Savior to the sinner, and then from the sinner to the Savior. The statement was complete; what more was there to add? But Paul could not leave the subject until he had voiced a splendid doxology: "Now unto the King eternal, incorruptible, invisible, the only God, be honour and glory for ever and ever. Amen." (1:17). It is hard to improve the stately cadence of successive adjectives in the Authorized Version: "eternal, immortal, invisible" (see also NIV); but there are several elements in this doxology not found on earlier occasions. The "King eternal" should perhaps be rendered "the King of ages" (RVM; RSV), a phrase founded on the psalmist's picture of the messianic kingdom as an everlasting kingdom (Ps. 145:13). It does not occur in any other Pauline passage, but was used once in the Revelation of John (Rev. 15:3). It employed a Jewish concept in order to acclaim Him as King of the age that now is and the age that is to come. The word rendered "immortal" (AV; RSV) is more literally rendered "incorruptible" in the Revised Version (Rom. 1:23). Perhaps a better word in English would be imperishable; that would harmonize with the thought in the other adjectives. The word *invisible* had been applied to God in a famous passage in the Epistle to the Colossians (Col. 1:15). This King is God alone, "the only God," a phrase of stark simplicity in keeping with Hebrew monotheism. To Him alone should be ascribed honor and glory, and this would be "for ever and ever," a phrase which marks the Hebrew idea of eternity. So Paul, chief of sinners, yet saved by grace, lifted up his heart in profound humility and in deepest worship to the king who is the only God and who is seen in His glorious majesty. Amen!

"This is good and acceptable in the sight of God our Saviour; who willeth that all men should be saved, and come to the knowledge of the truth. For there is one God, one mediator also between God and men, himself man, Christ Jesus, who gave himself a ransom for all."

I Timothy 2:3-5

Paul addressed Timothy in terms of deep personal affection at the end of the first chapter (1:18). Then he turned to the theme of church life and affairs, beginning with a remarkable exhortation to prayer. This exhortation could have sprung only from a man whose vision swept the world and tried to embrace all that he saw: "I exhort therefore, first of all, that supplications, prayers, intercessions, thanksgivings, be made for all men" (2:1). He saw that it was of primary importance that church members should learn to share in honest outreach toward all men. They were indeed to pray for each other, but they were to pray as well for Jew and gentile, for pagan and barbarian, for all men everywhere. Then he mentioned as a specific example the need to pray for all who were in authority: "for kings and all that are in high place" (2:2a). Such words, written at a time when Nero wore the imperial purple, provide a most interesting commentary on the New Testament attitude toward the State. It would moreover be for their own benefit to pray for their temporal overlords: "that we may lead a tranquil and quiet life in all godliness and gravity" (2:2b). The words *tranquil* and *quiet* were translated as quiet and peaceable in the Authorized Version. They were closely linked in meaning and point to a calm and settled spirit in the life of a nation or community. This would provide the right social environment for the cultivation of godliness and gravity, which conveys the twin ideas of personal devotion and Christian dignity. These will flourish best when law and order are maintained by earthly rulers in a strong and stable society.

Paul's next words sum up this counsel with a firm and direct affirmation: "This is good and acceptable in the sight of God our Saviour" (2:3). The first word, *this*, relates this verse to the exhortation to make prayer universal in its compass. Such prayer is both welcome and worthy; it is good in itself; it is acceptable to God. It is not a question of how we pray in the hearing of men; the one motive that counts is that it may be pleasing in the sight of God. It was perfectly natural for Paul to amplify his reference to God, and he did so by the use of a term that points to God's sovereign character and saving purpose for mankind. He made use of this identical appellation in the first verse of this letter: he was, he wrote, "an apostle of Christ Jesus according to the commandment of God our Saviour" (1:1). It was right to pray for all men because such prayer must be offered to God as our Savior. But just as Paul enlarged the name of God with the extra words *our Savior*, so he found in those words a fresh springboard for the development of his main theme. The verses that follow are an excellent example of Paul's gift for enforcing practical instruction with a doctrinal argument. A comparable illustration is the passage in the epistle to the church at Philippi in which Paul charged them to cultivate unity of heart and mind; and to strengthen that plain exhortation, he told them to let that mind be in them which was in Christ Jesus (Phil. 2:1–5). What was that mind? Paul answered that question in one of the richest statements on the person of

Christ ever written (Phil. 2:6–11). So it was here: Paul enforced his call for prayer by an appeal to the sovereign will and redeeming love of the God who was in Christ reconciling the world unto Himself (II Cor. 5:19).

It was in this incidental fashion that Paul introduced the next statement with its tremendous overtones: "who willeth that all men should be saved, and come to the knowledge of the truth" (2:4). The thought in this verse is strikingly similar to that in a Petrine statement: God is "not willing that any should perish, but that all should come to repentance" (II Peter 3:9, AV). The verb *willeth* has been better rendered desires (RSV) or wants (NIV). God's generous desire is that all men should come to a saving knowledge of God our Savior (2:3); that is why prayer should be made for all men (2:1). God is willing to be gracious to all, irrespective of class or sex or creed. This does not mean that all men will in fact be saved; it is not a doctrine that leads to universalism. But if man should be lost, he will be lost because he has used his freedom as a responsible person to turn away from God. The love of God is so magnanimous that it embraced the world in its compass; that love was seen as not sparing, but giving and sending His Son that all men might be saved. Whosoever believes on Him shall not perish, but shall have eternal life (John 3:16). God's great mercy reaches out to all men, but each man is a free moral agent. That is why this verse needs to be interpreted by the later comment: "We have our hope set on the living God, who is the Saviour of all men, specially of them that believe" (4:10). If men are to be saved, they must come to the place where they believe: this is fundamental to Paul's teaching, and he never ceased to declare that there is no alternative. This verse (2:4) does not refer specifically to the need to believe, but implies the same when speaking of coming to a knowledge of the truth, that is, to a recognition and understanding of the saving purpose of God revealed in and through Christ Jesus.

Paul's next words put forward an even more solid reason

for the cosmic outreach of the love and mercy of God: "For there is one God, one mediator also between God and men, himself man, Christ Jesus" (2:5). This is a more accurate translation, though less euphonious, than the Authorized Version: "For there is one God, and one mediator between God and men, the man Christ Jesus" (cf. RSV). There was a similar statement in an earlier Epistle: "Now a mediator is not a mediator of one; but God is one" (Gal. 3:20). Paul's theology was firmly grounded in the monotheism that marked Israel as unique among all the nations: "Hear, O Israel: the LORD our God is one LORD: and thou shalt love the LORD thy God with all thine heart" (Deut. 6:4–5). Let God be God, and let all the idols of the heathen perish. This was basic to Paul's doctrine that this God is the God of all the earth, and that His love reaches out to Jew and Gentile alike. But how is God's love to lay hold on us? How can a man who is defiled by sin find favor in His sight? That question seemed insoluble to Job when he voiced his lament: "There is no daysman betwixt us, That might lay his hand upon us both" (Job 9:33). But Paul had the answer: "There is one mediator between God and men" (RSV). The one true God sent His Son to become the middleman par excellence; He stands alone as the Mediator who can draw our broken lives back into union with God. Such a Mediator had to be made like us, sharing our flesh and blood. No angel in glory could have fulfilled that role. Therefore the text adds an emphatic description: Himself man, Christ Jesus. For the sixth time, the same order is observed: first the messianic title, then the name (1:1, 2, 12, 14, 15). This man was none other than the Christ, and His name was Jesus.

This verse paved the way for a further statement which set out the only ground on which the Mediator could effect His purpose: "who gave himself a ransom for all; the testimony to be borne in its own times" (2:6). This simple but comprehensive declaration lies at the heart of the gospel and holds the key to this passage. It is like an echo of the words of the

Lord Jesus: "The Son of man came . . . to give his life a ransom for many" (Mark 10:45). It was the same word, but in a compound form, and this was its only use in the Pauline writings. But the idea of a ransom was as well known to the Jews as to the Gentiles, and its meaning was plain. It was the price which had to be paid to purchase freedom for a captive or slave, and the person who was set free was then said to have been redeemed. The Lord Jesus gave Himself as a ransom of adequate merit or infinite value for the purchase of our freedom. The preposition was significant because the Greek word made it clear that this generous transaction was on behalf of all, and that word *all* rings out for the fourth and last time in this passage. The thrust of the sentence is that God is willing for all men to be saved, and has therefore paid a ransom in the person of His own Son which is available for all. Then if He gave Himself as a ransom for all, why are not all men saved? It is because not all avail themselves of the offered gift of freedom. They prefer to remain in the bondage from which they might have been redeemed. But the ransom was paid, and it was paid for all; and the testimony to that divine ransom was borne in its own times. The last clause is obscure, partly because the text is so compressed. There is a faint echo of the last words in a later saying: ". . . the appearing of our Lord Jesus Christ: which in its own times he shall shew . . ." (6:14–15). That testimony is everlasting in its significance for all men through the ages.

It was in order to spread this testimony that Paul became a herald of the gospel: "whereunto I was appointed a preacher and an apostle (I speak the truth, I lie not), a teacher of the Gentiles in faith and truth" (2:7). Paul could seldom resist the chance to speak about his vocation and ministry as a chosen servant of God. He could never forget that he ranked among the chief of sinners; but he could not ignore the fact that through God's grace he could also reckon himself to be the least of His servants. Paul had already emphasized his own special calling (1:1, 12), and he boldly affirmed that he was a

27

preacher and an apostle both by commandment and by appointment. Necessity had been laid on him, he could not help himself: ". . . for woe is unto me if I preach not the gospel" (I Cor. 9:16). The pronoun in the first person was emphatic: Paul could not get over his deep sense of wonder that he, even he, should have been chosen as a herald for Christ. This may explain why he felt moved to add the brief clause in parenthesis: "I speak the truth, I lie not." It was less for Timothy's benefit than for Paul's own inner reassurance that he made this vigorous assertion. It was in tune with a similar utterance made on another occasion: "I say the truth in Christ, I lie not" (Rom. 9:1; cf. II Cor. 11:31; Gal. 1:20). But this interruption did not disturb the flow of thought as Paul resumed the terms of self-designation: he was also "a teacher of the Gentiles in faith and truth." This was his favorite form of reference, and it served to confirm his claim that the gospel was for all men. Unto him was this grace given, that he should "preach among the Gentiles the unsearchable riches of Christ" (Eph. 3:8).

"And without controversy great is the mystery of godliness; He who was manifested in the flesh, justified in the spirit, seen of angels, preached among the nations, believed on in the world, received up in glory."

I Timothy 3:16

Paul had moved to an end of his treatment of the status of women (2:8–15), bishops (3:1–7), and deacons (3:8–13), and then paused to dwell on the needs of the church as a whole (3:14–15). This new section is personal in character: "These things write I unto thee, hoping to come unto thee shortly" (3:14). It was not so much that Timothy had been ignorant of the ground rules of church life and order as that Paul felt the need to confirm his former oral advice before his hoped-for coming in person. What Paul wrote would be made known in the church and would "buttress the authority" with which Timothy was invested.[1] This is further clarified in the words that follow: "but if I tarry long, that thou mayest know how men ought to behave themselves in the house of God . . ." (3:15). Paul could not be sure what length of time would elapse before he was free to make that journey. In the event of a prolonged delay, it was desirable that Timothy should understand what was required. He had to know how men ought to conduct themselves in the discharge of their duties

1. Guthrie, *Pastoral Epistles*, p. 87.

within the house of God. Paul had likened the church to a household in an earlier reference: "but if a man knoweth not how to rule his own house, how shall he take care of the church of God?" (3:5). The house of God is here seen as identical with "the church of the living God" (3:15). It is therefore not a building like the temple or a house made with hands; it refers to people, men and women whether Jew or Gentile, the whole congregation of all those who believe. There was one more phrase in apposition with what he had written about the church: "the pillar and ground of the truth" (3:15). This is better rendered "the pillar and bulwark of the truth" (RSV). One main task of "the church of the living God" in every age is that of a mainstay and bulwark of truth in the gospel.

Perhaps it was this last mention of truth that led to the spontaneous outburst of praise and magnificent testimony to the person of Christ. It was introduced by a formula designed to heighten the reader's expectation: "And without controversy, great is the mystery of godliness" (3:16). The expression "without controversy" was an emphatic assertion that this was a matter which lay beyond shadow of doubt. It would command universal consent so that not the mildest question would be raised as to its veracity. Paul had something great in mind, something both wonderful and amazing. He used the word *mystery* which had already occurred in an earlier sentence: "holding the mystery of the faith in a pure conscience" (3:9). Paul used this term in its technical character: it referred to something which was concealed from the knowledge of men until it pleased God to make it known by revelation. It was qualified in this text by the word *godliness* which had also appeared before: "that we may lead a tranquil and quiet life in all godliness and gravity" (2:2). But it had a much more personal character in this context, as the words that followed would show. The two words were joined in the phrase, "the mystery of godliness," an expression peculiar to this passage. But in another epistle, Paul had made use of the opposite expression: "the mystery of lawlessness" (II Thess. 2:7). The mystery of godliness was seen in the incarnation of the Son of God; the mystery of lawlessness will yet be seen in the incarnation of the man of sin. But to portray the mystery of godliness in this passage, Paul could resort only to the cadence and rhythm of a hymn whose lyrical quality shows the touch of genius in its origins in Greek.

So this opening formula, although written with a touch of grandeur, at once gave way to a far more splendid passage which sets out the Christology of the earliest believers. It is in the form of a hymn in which there are six lines arranged with the skill and symmetry of an oracle. This will be more clearly apprehended if they are set out as follows:

> He who was manifested in the flesh,
> justified in the spirit,
>> seen of angels,
>
> preached among the nations,
> believed on in the world,
>> received up in glory.

The whole stanza divides into two halves of three lines each; in each half two lines form a couplet which is then followed by the single indented line. The two sets of couplets and the single lines balance each other, and this sense of balance is made clear by the thought which each conveys. Thus what took place "in the flesh" is balanced by what took place "in the spirit"; the proclamation "among the nations" is balanced by the response "in the world"; the angel-watchers were balanced by the ascent into glory. It was something which could readily be committed to memory, and it can then be seen as a primitive confession of faith "which reads like a citation from canticle or catechism."[2] It starts with the incarnation and ends with the exaltation, though it is in language which partly unveils and partly conceals. It cannot be treated

2. Simpson, *Pastoral Epistles*, p. 60.

as a complete credal statement since there is no explicit reference to the cross and resurrection, but there can be no doubt that it was the language of worship and adoration.

The first couplet begins with a striking sentence on the incarnation: "He who was manifested in the flesh." The relative pronoun *who* undoubtedly refers to the Son of God in a way that marks out His preexistence. Other words in this clause recall certain Johannine expressions; the mystery of godliness was brought to light when the Word was made flesh (John 1:14). Divine revelation affords nothing so astonishing and inscrutable as the incarnate deity. This is clearly expressed in one of the stanzas of H. R. Bramley's hymn, "The Great God of Heaven Is Come Down to Earth":

> The Word in the bliss of the Godhead remains,
>   Yet in flesh comes to suffer the keenest of pains;
> He is that he was, and forever shall be,
>   But becomes that he was not, for you and for me.

It was in the fulness of time that God sent forth His Son to be born of a woman and cradled in a manger. He crossed every barrier in order to identify Himself with people like ourselves. He grew up as a child in an obscure and humble family; He became a man of sorrows who knew the bitter tang of poverty and need; and at last He tasted death for us all. He would neither try to avoid pain nor seek to evade death. It was by His own choice that He went to the cross where He suffered and died. But death could not hold Him; He broke through on the other side. It was as a result of that final triumph that He could be said to have been "justified in the spirit." He burst the bands of death and was "declared to be the Son of God" by that mighty demonstration of power (Rom. 1:4). The incarnation had its proper sequel in the resurrection. All His claims were vindicated; no one else was ever like Him; He was truly unique.

The second couplet begins with a succinct statement on the progress of the gospel: He was "preached among the nations." The Lord Jesus restricted His ministry to the lost sheep of the house of Israel, although there were isolated cases when He had contact with the Gentiles. Some individuals in Samaria and others in Decapolis made Him more than welcome; the centurion at Capernaum and the woman from Syro-Phoenicia had more faith than He had found in Israel; and there were Greeks who came seeking Jesus. But the standpoint for this statement was the resurrection when He gave the Twelve His command to "Go . . . and make disciples of all the nations" (Matt. 28:19). The Twelve were to bear witness to Him, starting at Jerusalem, spreading out to Judea and Samaria, and then reaching far beyond in order to touch the ends of the earth in His name. Paul had been called in a special manner to work among Gentiles and had risked his life on numerous occasions in his burning desire to proclaim the message of grace. This was an essential part of the mystery of which he spoke; the word itself was a technical term which he almost always used in connection with the Gentiles. God's hidden purpose was revealed at last in the coming of His Son, and the great open secret of the gospel was that Gentiles are as welcome as Jews to His mercy and grace. It was as a result of this moving discovery that Jesus could be said to be "believed on in the world." That statement was proleptical from the standpoint of the resurrection; it was like a vision of things to come. The Lord Jesus rejoiced in that vision. He foretold what must happen in the clearest language: "this gospel of the kingdom shall be preached in the whole world for a testimony unto all the nations; and then shall the end come" (Matt. 24:14).

The two single lines lift our eyes to an otherworldly level which must serve to enhance the mystery of godliness in our understanding: He was "seen of angels . . . received up in glory." There was a marked economy in the role of angels as far as the record of His earthly life was concerned. Angels were the heralds of the incarnation, and then of the resurrection. Apart from these two key events, there were only two

other recorded occasions of angelic ministry. Angels came
and waited on Him in the desert (Mark 1:13), and an angel
came and stood by His side in the garden (Luke 22:43). Jesus
knew that He needed only to call on His Father and a host of
angels would be at His command (Matt. 26:53); but He did
not, because He was content to live and die without angelic
intervention as we also must live and die. There were things
which the angels had desired to look into (I Peter 1:12); there
were other things that would be made known to the angels
by means of the church (Eph. 3:10). But when Christ rose
from the grave, He was seen of angels; they were the first to
see Him in the glory of the resurrection. His exaltation had
begun, and there was "joy in the presence of the angels of
God" (Luke 15:10). That joy would be immeasurably increased
when He was received up in glory. He stood on the Mount of
Olives in the midst of His friends with hands upraised to
bless; and while He was in the act of blessing, He began to ascend
before their eyes. He was removed as if by an unseen hand
and was taken up until a cloud received Him out of sight. All
the angels of God were there as an escort for the King of
Glory, and the everlasting doors on high were opened so that
He might go in. All heaven rejoiced as the incarnate Son of
God sat down at the right hand of the eternal majesty.

"If thou put the brethren in mind of these things, thou shalt be a good minister of Christ Jesus."

I Timothy 4:6-10

There was a marked alteration in the tone and tenor of Paul's letter once he concluded his lofty thoughts on the mystery of godliness. The gospel was worthy of all acceptation, but defeat would alternate with triumph in the story of its progress. He foresaw a dreadful decline from the simplicity of faith in Christ, and its first stage would be marked by a lapse from sound doctrine. This was not just something which he foretold from the vantage point of his own observation; it was something which the Holy Spirit had made known by express revelation. "But the Spirit saith expressly that in later times some shall fall away from the faith, giving heed to seducing spirits and doctrines of devils" (4:1). Apostasy would mean that its victims gave heed to spirits and doctrines that were false and wicked. "The main elements in their character"[1] were set out in somber language: "through the hypocrisy of men that speak lies, branded in their own conscience as with a hot iron" (4:2). Men who were "the dupes of evil spirits" would become the teachers of lies,[2] because their hypocrisy would deprive them of all sense of guilt and wrong in what they said or did. It would be as though their conscience were seared "with a hot iron"; they would be "past feeling" (Eph.

1. Guthrie, *Pastoral Epistles*, p. 92.
2. Simpson, *Pastoral Epistles*, p. 64.

4:19). Their false teaching would come to light in their negative attitude to marriage and diet; they would treat with
contempt the fact that God had appointed or created these
things that they might be ". . . received with thanksgiving by
them that believe and know the truth" (4:3). Paul then offered
his own reason for this great claim: it was based on the fact
that all that God made is good. Therefore they should receive
their food with thanksgiving, "for it is sanctified through the
word of God and prayer" (4:4–5).

Paul's next words directly addressed Timothy to seek to
encourage him. He would soon be required to cope with
false teaching: "If thou put the brethren in mind of these
things, thou shalt be a good minister of Christ Jesus, nourished in the words of the faith, and of the good doctrine
which thou hast followed until now" (4:6). Paul had already
exhorted Timothy to cultivate his own ministry with care:
"This charge I commit unto thee, my child Timothy, according to the prophecies which went before on thee, that by
them thou mayest war the good warfare" (1:18). His deep
concern was to insure that Timothy would understand the
charge for which he was responsible and would measure up
to the trust reposed in him. The phrase *to put in mind* was to
hint or suggest in a mild way; he was therefore to see that the
brethren were kept in mind of things which were "like
stepping stones over dangerous ground."[3] The brethren were
members of the congregation which had become his cure of
souls; this was probably in Ephesus. By keeping the brethren
informed, Timothy would prove himself a good minister of
Christ Jesus; a true servant of the messianic Savior. The
means to this end would be to keep up his own nurture in
"the words of the faith" (RSV); the body of doctrine as it had
been written no doubt by Paul's own hand. This was enlarged
by the additional remark about the sound doctrine which he
had learned from Paul himself and to which he had faithfully

3. Guthrie, *Pastoral Epistles*, p. 94.

adhered. Paul was moved to reiterate this call for true nurture in sound doctrine time and again; this is the nourishment that a good minister of Christ always requires.

Such good doctrine was the antidote to the influence of false teaching, irrespective of the quarter from which it might emanate: "but refuse profane and old wives' fables" (4:7). Paul was skilled in the use of such brief and pithy maxims in order to insure that his teaching would take effect. In sharp contrast with the doctrine in which Timothy was to nourish his faith, there were other things which called for decisive rejection. The word *refuse* was used elsewhere in these letters and called for a strong and total rejection. It was applied to a man who persisted in heresy: "A man that is heretical after a first and second admonition refuse" (Titus 3:10). It was also applied to the foolish questions that caused strife and debate: "foolish and ignorant questionings refuse, knowing that they gender strifes" (II Tim. 2:23). So Timothy was to reject what was profane, a word which had a slightly different connotation in Greek than in English. It was the reverse of what was sacred; to be profane would indicate an attitude of contempt or disdain toward the things of God. To take God's name in vain was to profane His name; it was to use His name in a light and careless spirit. It was not necessarily the same thing as modern profanity; it was exemplified in the case of Esau. He thought so little of his birthright that he sold it for a mess of pottage; he treated as common what should have been sacred (Heb. 12:16). So Timothy was warned against "the lawless and unruly, . . . the ungodly and sinners, . . . the unholy and profane" (1:9). He was also to reject old wives' fables, a phrase that sums up the foolish stories that passed from lip to lip. "Old wives" stands for those who were illiterate and superstitious, and the term brings out "the frivolous character of the false teachers."[4] Timothy was to reject all

4. Ibid., p. 95.

profane conversation and foolish stories; they were to be decisively refused.

Paul turned to an athletic metaphor in order to contrast the anemic influence of old wives' gossip with the far more healthy demands of disciplined exercise: ". . . And exercise thyself unto godliness: for bodily exercise is profitable for a little; but godliness is profitable for all things, having promise of the life which now is, and of that which is to come" (4:7–8). The verb *to exercise* had to do with training, and there is a further contrast between spiritual training and mere physical exercise. Timothy was to renounce all profane and foolish conversation in order to pursue the discipline of godliness. This was the third time this noble word was employed in this letter (see 2:2; 3:16), and the essential character of such authentic godliness was as clear as daylight. Physical exercise is not without its place, but it profits only for a little; that is, either within certain limits or for a time (see James 4:14). Because our bodies are mortal, they cannot be sustained by discipline or exercise beyond our life span. But godliness is durable in time and for eternity; its values are everlasting. It holds promise for the life that now is because it adds strength to character and helps us to weather all storms. It also holds promise for the life yet to come because it points us to heaven and determines our destiny. The first point was well summed up by the later saying: "godliness with contentment is great gain" (6:6). Those words referred particularly to the life that now is, for he went on to say: "we brought nothing into the world, . . . neither can we carry anything out; but having food and covering, we shall be therewith content" (6:7–8). But there is more, much more. Authentic godliness outlasts time and endures forever.

Paul again made use of his new and impressive formula to underline the importance of what he had to say: "Faithful is the saying, and worthy of all acceptation" (4:9). This is identical with the form in which it was employed on the earlier occasion (1:15), and it is the only context in which it is reproduced exactly. It has often been thought that this particular saying refers back to what Paul said concerning godliness, partly because that verse reads more like a proverb than the words that follow. But it seems more likely that the next sentence was clearly in view, for that sentence carried far more weight as a word of sound doctrine. By its very contents it attracts natural emphasis, and an initial formula would help to clothe it with suitable dignity. It was in this way and for this purpose that this impressive formula was employed before: it was as a solemn preface to words which were truly memorable. Therefore we may assume that there was a momentary pause at the end of the last verse; it was as though Paul stood still in his tracks.

Then Paul began again and made use of these words to alert Timothy to what he next intended to write: "Faithful is the saying, and worthy of all acceptation." Dignity and gravity are mingled in that saying; it can hardly fail to make us aware that Paul's words came from his heart. He claimed Timothy's hearing and response in advance; he sought to awaken all that was sensitive in Timothy's understanding. What he was about to write could be relied on as true and faithful; it deserved to win universal acceptance. What more could Paul have done to stimulate interest and encourage attention? Did Timothy need anything more to focus his mind on what he was reading?

Paul's words identified himself with the recipient of his letter and read like a personal confession of faith and hope: "For to this end we labour and strive, because we have our hope set on the living God, who is the Saviour of all men, specially of them that believe" (4:10). The first use of the formula to introduce a faithful saying had been followed by the word *that* (or because) leaving no doubt as to what Paul meant to impress on his readers (1:15). But the formula on this occasion was followed by the conjunction *for*, as if to supply a reason for the claim that the saying was reliable. But it seems best to treat the first phrase as a whole, and to relate it to what Paul had been saying about godliness. This is confirmed by the continued metaphor drawn from strenuous exercise such as would be involved in the training of an athlete or a gymnast. The phrase *labor and strive* offers a clear picture of a man who would wear himself out with toil and fatigue and would strive to the point of physical agony in order to attain the goal. The pursuit of godliness is like a race that demands every ounce of strength we can command. The grand motive for such rigorous endeavor is a hope that is fixed in God. Paul's use of the perfect tense was deliberate: "we have fixed, and still fix" our hope in "the living God" (cf. 3:15). Later Paul would encourage Timothy to charge men not to set their hope on uncertain riches, ". . . but on God, who giveth us richly all things to enjoy" (6:17). This God is the Savior of all men; His providence and government help to preserve the just and the unjust. But that idea is raised to a higher level with a special implication in the words Paul at once went on to add: "specially of them that believe."

"Neglect not the gift that is in thee, which was given thee by prophecy, with the laying on of the hands of the presbytery."

I Timothy 4:11-16

At this point, the exhortation became more personal; it was addressed even more directly to Timothy. It was one thing for Paul to give Timothy general directions for the exercise of his ministry; it was a great deal more to speak to him about his own needs if he were to develop into "a good minister of Christ Jesus" (4:6). Paul knew Timothy's natural diffidence; he was determined to strengthen Timothy's hands. Paul wanted to encourage Timothy to act without hesitancy and to speak with authority. This required firm and unfaltering purpose; it needed the moral strength and courage of an absolute reliance on God. This is implied in the crisp words which begin this passage: "These things command and teach" (4:11). What things? The same things Paul spoke of when he began this section: "If thou put the brethren in mind of these things" (4:6). He meant things such as apostasy and hypocrisy; prohibitions about marriage and diet; profane and foolish stories. He meant as well things such as he had enjoined Timothy to cultivate: concern for sound doctrine, the discipline of godliness, and a hope fixed in God. E. K. Simpson asks a rhetorical question: would the reward for such spiritual training, such labor and fatigue, be commensurate with the effort it required? And he answered, Assuredly; since their eyes were fastened on things whose value is everlasting.[1] "We look not at the things which are seen, but at the things which are not seen: for the things which are seen are temporal; but the things which are not seen are eternal" (II Cor. 4:18). Timothy was to impart to others the things which he had himself been taught; he was to command and instruct as one who could speak with authority.

Therefore Timothy was not to undervalue himself in the presence of those who may have been older: "Let no man despise thy youth; but be thou an ensample to them that believe, in word, in manner of life, in love, in faith, in purity" (4:12). *Youth* was a term which spread itself over an even wider age-range in classical times than is the case today. Perhaps fifteen years had elapsed since Paul's first visit to Lystra when he had found Timothy (Acts 16:1). Timothy was old enough to join Paul and Silas on their second journey two or three years later. It seems safe to assume that at the time when Paul wrote this letter, Timothy was not less than thirty-five years old.[2] But in the eyes of the local elders, he was still a young man; he was still young enough to need to "flee youthful lusts" (II Tim. 2:22). The people were accustomed to the veteran leadership of Paul; it may have been hard for them to accept Timothy as Paul's substitute. Therefore Paul wanted to strengthen Timothy's hands: "Let no man despise thy youth." There was decisive emphasis on the word *despise*, for Paul well knew that Greek culture held youth to be subordinate to age. He gave similar instruction concerning Timothy to the church at Corinth: "if Timothy come, see that he be with you without fear; for he worketh the work of the Lord, as I also do; let no man therefore despise him" (I Cor. 16:10–11). Paul would offer the same encouragement when he wrote to Titus: "Let no man despise thee" (Titus 2:15). The best antidote to that dilemma was to

---

1. Simpson, *Pastoral Epistles*, p. 69.
2. See the chronological table in R. D. Shaw, *The Pauline Epistles*, p. XI.

cultivate a life which would be an example to all; this was what Paul himself aspired to do (cf. Phil. 3:17; II Thess. 3:9). Paul then mentioned five marks of such a life: careful conversation, godly conduct, charity, faithfulness, and a blameless spirit. Such a life would invest Timothy with authority that had nothing to do with age; it would be that of a man of God who dwelt in their midst.

The disciplines of character were to go hand in hand with diligence in ministry: "Till I come, give heed to reading, to exhortation, to teaching" (4:13). Was Paul writing to Timothy in Ephesus from some other city in the Levant? (cf. 1:3). There is little doubt that he was planning another visit as soon as it could be arranged. The phrase "till I come" was in full accord with Paul's declared purpose: "These things write I unto thee, hoping to come unto thee shortly" (3:14). Paul could not say how long Timothy would have to wait for his arrival; meanwhile Timothy was to give heed to three special aspects of his appointed ministry. First of all, he was to give heed to reading, a word that was broad enough to take in all forms of reading. But the obvious reference is to reading aloud, reading to others, reading in public. It was customary to read the Old Testament in the synagogue, and this custom carried over into the church. Public reading of the Scriptures became one of the most basic features of the worship of an ordinary congregation. In an age when many converts were illiterate slaves, this reading of Scripture in the congregation was the one way in which they could come to know that Word which could make them "wise unto salvation" (II Tim. 3:15). Therefore no care was too great to insure that the Scriptures were read with clarity and sympathy. This would provide a firm base for exhortation and for teaching, words which refer to preaching and doctrine. The reading of Scripture led to exhortation and exposition so that members of the church could be stirred to a fitting response. Preaching alone was not enough when it was mainly hortatory;

instruction was just as essential so that truth could be firmly implanted in mind and memory.

Paul then pointedly reminded Timothy of the origin of his ministry: "Neglect not the gift that is in thee, which was given thee by prophecy, with the laying on of the hands of the presbytery" (4:14). To be always mindful of a spiritual landmark in the past may not be easy, but to forget leads to neglect. So Timothy was admonished not to neglect the gift that was in him. What gift was that? Paul did not write in more precise terms about its nature; the word itself was a favorite expression in his letters. But at the least, it was something spiritual; he may even have meant that such a gift which was "in thee" was God's Holy Spirit. The thought in Paul's mind was enlarged by two further statements about facts which confirmed this gift. The first was the fact that it had been "given . . . by prophecy." It is clear that prophecy was an element which figured prominently in Timothy's original calling, though it was not mentioned by Luke in the Acts. Paul had written: "This charge I commit unto thee, my child Timothy, according to the prophecies which went before on thee" (1:18). The history and character of these prophecies remain obscure, but they must have taken the form of a prediction pointing to Timothy's future career. At any rate, this was accompanied by "the laying on of the hands of the presbytery." Paul's next letter referred to this imposition of hands in a way that suggests that he acted alone in the ordination of his son in the faith: "I put thee in remembrance that thou stir up the gift of God, which is in thee through the laying on of my hands" (II Tim. 1:6). Perhaps Paul was the main person involved, while the elders joined him in that solemn moment. It is worthwhile to note that the laying on of hands was accompanied by the gift of the Holy Spirit in Paul's own experience (Acts 9:17; cf. 8:17; 19:6).

In what spirit was Timothy to cultivate the gift that was in him? Paul left him in no doubt: "Be diligent in these things; give thyself wholly to them; that thy progress may be manifest unto all" (4:15). The word translated "be diligent" is not only uncommon, but is also capable of more than one shade of meaning. It may mean to meditate; it may mean to exercise oneself. The idea of meditation is strengthened by comparison with its use in compound form in another context: "Settle it therefore in your hearts, not to meditate beforehand how to answer" (Luke 21:14). The two meanings have been combined in this paraphrastic reading: Be diligent. Timothy was to give his wholehearted attention to "these things." What things? The phrase had already been used twice in this chapter (4:6, 11). But here it referred particularly to the things Paul had just mentioned (4:12–14). He wrote with a sense of compelling urgency; this led him to endorse his words with a further summons to give himself wholly to them. He was to give himself without reserve; to devote all his energies to them. He was to be immersed in them as the body in the air that it breathes.[3] There could be no slacking, no idle leisure, and no diminution of resolve. He was so to live that his progress, his spiritual development, would be seen and marked by all. His life would be under constant observation; many eyes would watch and assess him. He might not like it, but could not prevent it; observing and assessing others has always been part of the pattern of life and it affects all men. Therefore it was vital that his manner of life should be such that it would commend the Lord Jesus and adorn His doctrine. Men would judge this for themselves in the light of the progress they saw.

The whole passage closes with a final exhortation equally relevant to Timothy's character and his ministry: "Take heed to thyself, and to thy teaching. Continue in these things; for in doing this thou shalt save both thyself and them that hear thee" (4:16). Paul had already exhorted Timothy to give heed to the leading features of his public activity with the congregation (4:13); but that was not enough. This fresh call was at

3. Guthrie, *Pastoral Epistles*, p. 99.

once both more personal and more demanding. Timothy was to take heed to his manner of life and to the tenor of his teaching. He was to keep a strict eye on himself and was to be equally vigilant about the truth he was called to impart. There could be no room for discrepancy between his way of life and the doctrine he taught. Personal holiness was the basic prerequisite for all effective ministry. This was reminiscent of Paul's farewell address to the elders of Ephesus at Miletus: "Take heed therefore unto yourselves, and to all the flock, over the which the Holy Ghost hath made you overseers" (Acts 20:28, KJV). Therefore Timothy was to continue, to persist, to persevere, in his pursuit of these twin goals. The phrase about "these things" was employed for the fourth time in this chapter (see 4:6, 11, 15); its scope and sweep were as wide as the themes of which Paul wrote. But Paul had one more thing to say. Timothy was summoned to guard his manner of life and the doctrine he taught because he was always to be mindful of his hearers. Failure on his part in either area would destroy his influence and deny his instruction. He was so to act that he would save not only himself, but also his hearers; for the ultimate salvation of both teacher and hearers was the one thing Paul so greatly desired.

*"I charge thee in the sight of God, and
Christ Jesus, and the elect angels, that thou
observe these things without prejudice,
doing nothing by partiality."*

I Timothy 5:21-25

A new section begins with this chapter; it is mainly concerned with advice on matters dealing with the welfare of a congregation. Paul spoke as a veteran whose long experience could guide Timothy through the shoals of proper conduct toward various groups of church members. Paul was mindful of Timothy's comparative youthfulness; it was therefore common sense to counsel him to act with proper respect toward those who were older and with natural dignity toward those who were younger (5:1-2). But that was a fairly general observation, and Paul moved on at once to the case of widows. It is clear that widows had been a source of real anxiety from the early days of the church onward (see Acts 6:1). Timothy was to cultivate a spirit of sympathetic insight toward those who were "widows indeed" (5:3), those who had lost both their husband and their means of support. Careful regulations were necessary in order to act wisely toward those who would be "recipients of the church's bounty" (5:3-8).[1] This led Paul to speak of those who could be enrolled in a special class as widows. It is not clear whether Paul was speaking of a special order of those who

1. Guthrie, *Pastoral Epistles*, p. 100.

47

could perform certain specified ministries in the congregation. At all events, a fixed age was desirable and their duties would be charitable (5:9–10). Younger widows were eligible for relief, but could not be employed in a formal capacity as they might still marry again (5:11–16). Paul then turned to elders as those who were leaders in the congregation. Generous provision should be made for their need, and they should be properly protected from false accusation. Any complaint ought to be formally lodged so that justice could be seen by all (5:17–20).

All these regulations for widows and elders came to a halt with an unexpected personal exhortation: "I charge thee in the sight of God, and Christ Jesus, and the elect angels, that thou observe these things without prejudice, doing nothing by partiality" (5:21). These sudden and solemn words of adjuration were designed to overcome Timothy's natural diffidence in dealing with sensitive areas of church activity. E. K. Simpson says that the word *to charge* had been used as a term of grave protest in the Attic lawcourts.[2] So Paul issued this most solemn protest "in the sight of [that is, before] God, and Christ Jesus, and the elect angels." Paul would employ almost the same form of exhortation again in his final letter: "I charge thee in the sight of God, and of Christ Jesus" (II Tim. 4:1). But there was no mention of "the elect angels" in this later address; it was unusual even in the context of this verse where it might be an echo of his earlier reference to God "who was manifested in the flesh, justified in the spirit, seen of angels" (3:16). Elect angels are those who kept their first estate and who are the unseen watchers of God's unfolding providence in the affairs of men. What then was the object of this weighty exhortation? It was that Timothy should be strict to observe these things; that is, the rules about the widows and elders in the congregation. This Timothy was to do in a special spirit; he was to act without prejudice and without

2. Simpson, *Pastoral Epistles*, p. 79.

48

partiality. He was never to let personal preference slant his thinking or color his judgment. He was to be just and even-handed in all these things.

This led to a further emphatic injunction on the subject of the choice of elders: "Lay hands hastily on no man, neither be partaker of other men's sins: keep thyself pure" (5:22). The first instance of the laying on of hands was in the case of the seven men "of good report" who were chosen to assist the apostles in Jerusalem (Acts 6:3). The leaders of the church in Antioch "laid their hands" on Barnabas and Saul on the eve of the first missionary journey (Acts 13:3). Paul and Barnabas appointed elders in the churches they had planted (Acts 14:23). And Paul laid his hands on Timothy in a solemn rite of ordination (I Tim. 4:14; II Tim. 1:6). It is reasonable to take this verse as a sensible direction which would protect Timothy from mistaken decisions in the choice of elders. Nothing was to be done without proper care and forethought; there should be no undue haste or impulsive commitment. Ordination was a solemn matter for the one who was to ordain as well as for the one who was to be ordained. Timothy was to act as a responsible leader in the choice of elders and the imposition of hands. This was joined with a stark summons not to partake in the sins of others. This seems to mean that if he were careless in matters of ordination, he would be held accountable for the sins of the men whom he ordained. It could hardly be more solemn as a warning against undue haste in the choice or the ordination of men who were marked out for some spiritual office. This may explain the rather abrupt clause with which the verse concludes: "keep thyself pure." Timothy would need to act in such a way that the church would see him as an honorable servant of God. If he were to ordain men who were pure, it was imperative that his life should be no less pure.

The next verse comes as a surprise, but throws light on Timothy's character: "Be no longer a drinker of water, but use a little wine for thy stomach's sake and thine often infirmities" (5:23). Paul recognized that Timothy lacked a robust constitution; he was handicapped by a delicate state of health which might have disinclined him to take a strict line toward others. Paul was eager on the one hand to give Timothy's sense of duty and purpose the strength of steel; on the other hand, Paul was genuinely considerate for Timothy's chronic infirmity. Therefore while Paul enjoined him to cultivate purity of heart and life, he was concerned that Timothy should not react in an ascetic direction. Paul spoke as a veteran traveler; he knew all the hazards from his own long experience. His instruction was practical and down to earth; he would discourage Timothy from drinking water. Paul could hardly have known that ailments such as dysentery and hepatitis are incurred by drinking contaminated water; he was still less likely to have known that water has to be boiled before it is safe for drinking. Common sense and experience taught him that it was best to abstain from water and to drink "a little wine" for medicinal reasons. E. K. Simpson notes that Plutarch prescribed wine for stomach ailments,[3] and Paul recommended it to Timothy as a tonic for health. It is significant that Paul had to contend with a thorn in the flesh and that Timothy was often afflicted with infirmities. Neither was healed from that physical affliction; they were both called to live and work by the grace of God within the limits of such strength as they had.

After that brief parenthesis with its fatherly instruction, Paul went on with the line of thought which had been in his mind from the outset: "Some men's sins are evident, going before unto judgment; and some men also they follow after" (5:24). Paul had already placed on Timothy a strong caution not to lay hands lightly on those who were seeking spiritual office, and that charge was now reinforced by a statement on the need for accurate assessment of motive and conduct.

3. Ibid., p. 80.

Not all men come from the same mold, even when they are one in sin. In the case of some men, sin is self-evident; no one is left in doubt as to their way of life. They sin boldly, and their sin goes before "unto judgement." In the case of others, sin is less apparent; it lies below the surface and is found in the dark corners of subtle obstinacy or hidden hypocrisy. Men love darkness rather than light because things that are evil flourish in the dark. It is always easier to sin under the cloak of night than in the broad light of the day. The darkness hides, no one sees; who will know? Those are the men whose sins follow after. What is done in secret will be proclaimed from the housetop. Judgment will come on the known and on the unknown sinner alike. Timothy would not need to hesitate in the case of the known sinner, but might have to reserve judgment in the case of others. How accurate his assessment of godliness or godlessness might be would be made clear in the day of judgment when the secrets of all hearts are made known. Meanwhile, there could be no escape from the heavy burden involved in the need to assess men for spiritual office in the congregation.

But Paul did not conclude on the note of sin and judgment; he went on to speak of good works and their proper recognition: "In like manner also there are good works that are evident; and such as are otherwise cannot be hid" (5:25). Paul did not speak of good works in contrast to faith; that was not in question. It was not his purpose to praise good works as a source of merit, as though they could earn God's favor for the man who did them. But he could not be too insistent in his emphasis on good works as the proof that a man was truly regenerate. Grace had to issue in a godly manner of life; doctrine was bound to walk hand-in-hand with conduct. Therefore this verse is a natural counterpart in thought and in structure to the last verse. What is true of sin is no less true of good works; they are often self-evident. There are many humble men and women who think nothing about themselves, but whose good works shine like a light before the eyes of all. The love of God is in their hearts; it must find an outlet in what they do. They are guileless in motive and action; their goodness is sterling in its reality and worth. There are others whose good works are done in secret; they do not let their right hand know what the left hand has done. What they do may be known only in part while they are yet alive; but it *cannot be hid.* They rest from their labors, and their work still lives on. The day will come when the truth is declared, and the King will make them welcome: "Inasmuch as ye did it unto one of these my brethren, even these least, ye did it unto me" (Matt. 25:40).

"But godliness with contentment is great gain."

I Timothy 6:6-10

The last chapter in this letter begins with an exhortation to servants and masters who were fellow members of the congregation (cf. Titus 2:9-14). This was a theme which Paul felt bound to take up with the churches in Ephesus and Colossae (Eph. 6:5-9; Col. 3:22—4:1); but his remarks in this case were confined to slaves. Slaves and owners stood on equal ground when they were saved by grace through faith in Christ alone. But that spiritual equality did not apply to their status in the daily affairs of a household. Some slaves served in non-Christian households; they were so to act that there would be no reproach on their account against "the name of God and the doctrine" which they believed. Other slaves whose masters belonged to the congregation might be tempted to neglect their duties; they would need to avoid any conduct that took improper advantage of their masters (6:1-2). Then Paul went on to say something further about those who were false teachers. The test would be whether their teaching was in accord with ". . . sound words, even the words of our Lord Jesus Christ, and . . . the doctrine which is according to godliness" (6:3). Those teachers whose doctrine did not measure up to that test were then dismissed in terms of scorn. They were puffed up in spite of an abysmal ignorance; they suffered the disease of argument and wordiness; they had fallen into the snare of strife and envy, wrangling and fantasy; they had come to suppose that godliness was a way of gain. This was the sin which beset Simon Magus; the false teachers gave it a new twist. They tried to use their own garrulous profession of faith as a means for material profit (6:4–5).

Paul turned away from false teachers and their sordid motives in order to conclude with a positive emphasis on those rules of life which are of universal significance: "But godliness with contentment is great gain" (6:6). Godliness is one of Paul's favorite expressions used in the pastoral Epistles; it is indeed strange that it is not found anywhere else in the New Testament apart from four verses in II Peter (1:3, 6, 7; 3:11). It is found eight times in this letter (2:2; 3:16; 4:7, 8; 6:3, 5, 6, 11), and once each in Titus and II Timothy (Titus 1:1; II Tim. 3:5). With the exception of one occasion when Paul spoke of "the mystery of godliness" (3:16), the word *godliness* was always used to denote a man's manner of life in its Godward aspect. It speaks of gravity and piety of character in relation to God; the godly man is one whose life is centered in and controlled by the love and fear of God. In this verse, it is linked with *contentment,* a word which is only found twice as a noun. Paul used it in his reassurance for the church at Corinth: "God is able to make all grace abound unto you; that ye, having always all sufficiency [contentment] in everything, may abound unto every good work" (II Cor. 9:8). It also appears once as an adjective: "I have learned, in whatsoever state I am, therein to be content" (Phil. 4:11). It may mean to be self-sufficient or independent, and it is a virtue of the highest value. Neither complacent nor complaining, but contented; neither ambitious nor dependent, but contented: such is the man who is activated by a godly spirit. This is great gain, in stark contrast with those who thought an appearance of godliness would prove a way of gain (6:5). "Godliness is profitable for all things" (4:8): it is independent of circumstances and constant in value in time and for eternity.

Paul then backed up this line of thought with an axiom

drawn from the Old Testament: "for we brought nothing into the world, for neither can we carry anything out" (6:7). This has its root in Job's amazing expression of faith in the midst of almost total destitution. In one day he lost all that he had; yet he did not curse the desert brigands who had pillaged his flocks, nor the wretched servants who were now dead as a result of their failure to watch, nor the young men who had been slain with the edge of the sword. His sons and his daughters had all died in a storm which brought the roof of the house down on their heads. Job was stripped of his possessions and his family, yet he would not accuse God of any dreadful improvidence. Job's personal agony was all the more profound because his faith stood fast, and it was that faith which moved him to exclaim: "Naked came I out of my mother's womb, and naked shall I return thither: the LORD gave, and the LORD hath taken away; blessed be the name of the LORD" (Job 1:21). Those words have echoed down the ages and have found a response in the hearts of thousands. Solomon repeated the same theme when he spoke of the riches which will perish: "As he came forth of his mother's womb, naked shall he go again as he came, and shall take nothing for his labour, which he may carry away in his hand" (Eccles. 5:15). Therefore Paul could take up the same thought with telling effect and quote it in support of his claim about godliness and contentment. We brought nothing into this world, and we will carry nothing out; material gain was irrelevant at our birth, and will be no less irrelevant when we die.

On the basis of that Old Testament quotation, Paul drew his own logical conclusion: "but having food and covering we shall be therewith content" (6:8). We come naked into the world; we go naked out of the world: therefore if we have food and raiment during our lifetime, we ought to be more than content. Food and raiment are the barest necessities; to have them is enough. Food stood for the simple diet that meets daily hunger; raiment was the homemade clothing of the ordinary workman. Jacob vowed before God at Bethel after his dream: "If God will be with me, and will keep me in this way that I go, and will give me bread to eat, and raiment to put on, so that I come again to my father's house in peace, then shall the LORD be my God" (Gen. 28:20–21). Paul's formula for contentment in this verse must recall the words in the Sermon on the Mount: "Be not therefore anxious, saying, What shall we eat? or, What shall we drink? or, Wherewithal shall we be clothed?" (Matt. 6:31). Food and raiment belong to the present order of things, and our Father knows that we have need of these things. The man who seeks first the kingdom of God must trust God to add all other things which may be truly needful. It was in this spirit that John Wesley wrote to George Whitefield from Georgia in 1737, urging him to go out to that infant colony. "Only Mr. Delamotte is with me, till God shall stir up the hearts of some of His servants who, putting their lives in His hands, shall come over and help us. What if thou art the man, Mr. Whitefield? Do you ask what you shall have? Food to eat and raiment to put on; a house to lay your head in, such as your Lord had not; and a crown of glory that fadeth not away."[1] Whitefield read that letter and his heart leaped within; before the end of the year, he was on his way.

There was a stern contrast between those who led a godly life and those who set their hearts on earthly gain: "But they that desire to be rich fall into a temptation and a snare and many foolish and hurtful lusts, such as drown men in destruction and perdition" (6:9). There are many warnings in Scripture about the fatal pursuit of wealth when it is seen as an end in itself; these warnings are equally as relevant in the society to which we now belong as in the world in which Paul lived. But Paul did not write in condemnation of wealth as such, nor of those in whose hands wealth resided. Those who are rich as a result of inheritance or reward are liable to temptations of a subtle nature. It is easy for them to put their

1. J. R. Andrews, *George Whitefield*, p. 25.

trust in their riches and to think that they have need of nothing: hence how hard it must be for those that have riches to enter the kingdom of God! But Paul's warning in this context was aimed at those who were obsessed with an inordinate desire to amass wealth. "They that desire to be rich" can think of nothing that does not help them to achieve that end. They are mastered by the lure of money: the more they have, the more they want to get. They do not use their wealth as good stewards who must one day render up an account; they are deceived by it until in the end it chokes them. But that is the first stage on the road to ruin; the next is when they fall into the power of the tempter, and "the snare of the devil" (3:7; II Tim. 2:26), and many other foolish cravings and hurtful passions. This lust for wealth will at last drown those whom it swamps. Paul chose a verb often applied to ships at sea; it pointed to shipwreck, total loss, destruction and perdition.

One might have thought that Paul had now spoken strongly enough, but he went on to drive his point home with one more emphatic sentence: "For the love of money is a root of all kinds of evil: which some reaching after have been led astray from the faith, and have pierced themselves through with many sorrows" (6:10). The love, or lure, or lust that the pursuit of wealth inspires is one of those seminal obsessions which breeds as its offspring all manner of evil. Paul said that it was a root, a disastrously fruitful root, of all kinds of evil. Those who try to serve both God and mammon like Ananias and Sapphira are caught in a web of wrong feeling, wrong thinking, wrongdoing, from which they can seldom escape. They become selfish, grasping, worldly, deceitful, covetous, dishonest: it would not be hard to list more of the many kinds of evil to which moneygrubbers are prey. It is impossible to nurse the love of God and the love of the world in the same heart at the same time. Those who mistakenly succumb to the love of money, reaching after worldly gains and material comforts at the expense of true spiritual

57

aspiration, have already begun to go astray and to renounce the faith they once professed. What more was necessary for Paul to say? It was as though he could scarcely find words trenchant enough for his purpose. He was ready to add metaphor to metaphor in order to drive home the lesson. Those who set their hearts on money are in danger of becoming like Saul who fell on his own sword to die of shame and sorrow: they pierce themselves through with many sorrows and are likely to die from the "self-inflicted pangs"[2] which the cares of this world must always entail. Grim and ugly will be their fate.

2. Guthrie, *Pastoral Epistles*, p. 114.

"But thou, O man of God, flee these things; and follow after righteousness, godliness, faith, love, patience, meekness."

I Timothy 6:11-16

Paul turned from his picture of the dire fate in store for those who set their hearts on the love of money to address himself once more in a very personal way to Timothy: "But thou, O man of God, flee these things; and follow after righteousness, godliness, faith, love, patience, meekness" (6:11). He would repeat the same exhortation, and in almost the same words, in his last letter: "But flee youthful lusts, and follow after righteousness, faith, love, peace, with them that call on the Lord out of a pure heart" (II Tim. 2:22). Paul's use of the personal pronoun *thou* was emphatic in order to sharpen the contrast with what had gone before. It was strengthened by the use of an old Hebrew appellation in a direct appeal: "O man of God." This was a form of address which would remind Timothy of "his high vocation and lineage.";[1] he was indeed called to stand in the line of the ancient prophets. Therefore he was to flee from what was wrong, never to court even the least transient temptation. Paul used the same general formula, "these things," to sum up what he had in mind; it must refer to the things which he had listed and which are the result of false teaching and wrong conduct (6:3–5). But while Timothy was to flee from things in one quarter, he was called

1. Simpson, *Pastoral Epistles*, p. 87.

to follow after things in another direction. This antithesis was truly Pauline in style and was repeated exactly in his final letter (II Tim. 2:22). The objects of pursuit were grouped in three brackets; they sum up the virtues which ought to mark the man of God. Righteousness and godliness spoke for themselves; faith and love were basic to Paul's teaching; patience and meekness sprang from likeness to Christ.

The call to flee some things and to follow others led at once to an equally vigorous summons to fight for and lay hold on something further: "Fight the good fight of the faith, lay hold on the life eternal, whereunto thou wast called, and didst confess the good confession in the sight of many witnesses" (6:12). This verse begins like an echo of the earlier injunction to "war the good warfare" (1:18). Paul's language was often colored by these "soldierly metaphors," and the martial ring of this clause is clear and strong.[2] Timothy had begun to fight that good fight of faith, and he was to keep on as he had begun. It was *the faith* of which Paul spoke, the creed as it were of apostolic teaching, and in solemn contrast with the false faith of those who had tampered with the gospel. The next summons, "to lay hold on," was an aorist imperative which spoke of a single event. Timothy's continued battle to guard the faith was linked with the personal assurance of the life eternal on which he had laid hold with a grasp that he would never relax. It was to this end that Timothy had been called and had "confessed the good confession." The verb and the noun have the same repetitive ring as in the call to fight the good fight. It is not clear to what event those words pointed, but it must have been well-known since it was "in the sight of many witnesses." The Book of Acts records that when Paul found Timothy on his second missionary journey, Timothy "was well reported of by the brethren that were at Lystra and Iconium" (Acts 16:2). They had seen Timothy's manner of life and could testify to his

2. Ibid.

confession of faith. Paul's clear words of recollection were therefore an encouragement.

This led Paul to a more importunate exhortation which was to grow into one of his most splendid doxologies: "I charge thee in the sight of God, who quickeneth all things, and of Christ Jesus, who before Pontius Pilate witnessed the good confession" (6:13). Although a new verb in the Greek text was employed, this verse invites comparison with the solemn injunction Paul had already given: "I charge thee in the sight of God, and Christ Jesus, and the elect angels . . ." (5:21). The phrase "in the sight of God, and Christ Jesus," was now exactly repeated, but each segment in the phrase was amplified. He called God to witness as the one who "quickeneth all things;" who gives life and breath to all that lives and moves. This was clearly meant to allude to what he had written about life eternal (6:12). God alone is the Author and Giver of life, and is therefore ever watchful over those whom He has quickened. Paul then referred to Christ Jesus who witnessed a good confession in the presence of Pontius Pilate. This also clearly referred to what Paul had written about Timothy's confession (6:12). Paul often invoked the name of God as a witness to the truth of what Paul had said (see Rom. 1:9; II Cor. 1:23; Phil. 1:8; I Thess. 2:5, 10); but this verse is almost unique in his letters as an invocation of Christ as a witness. It refers to that momentous interview with the Roman procurator during His trial. Was He a king, and if so, what sort of a king? "To this end have I been born and to this end have I come into the world," He said, ". . . that I should bear witness unto the truth. Every one that is of the truth heareth my voice" (John 18:37). This was the good confession of that true and faithful witness, and it was sealed by His death on the cross.

But what was the special burden laid on Timothy in this solemn exhortation? It is shown in the next words: "that thou keep the commandment, without spot, without reproach, until the appearing of our Lord Jesus Christ" (6:14). Paul could not hide his deep concern for this son in the faith; he longed for Timothy's steadfast continuance in the life and testimony to which he was already committed. Therefore Timothy was to keep the commandment which had been laid on him. This is sufficiently indefinite to allow a wider application than the immediate context requires; but its primary reference must be to the very personal injunction Paul had just voiced (6:11–12). It bears comparison with Paul's final urgent appeal: "O Timothy, keep that which is committed unto thee" (6:20). The two descriptive adjectives *without spot* and *without reproach*, are best applied to Timothy himself rather than to the commandment; and they serve to underline earlier demands that he should keep himself pure and should take heed to himself. The word rendered without spot or unstained was rare, and for that reason all the more impressive. Timothy would be encouraged if he were to conduct himself as one who was ever mindful of the ultimate "appearing of our Lord Jesus Christ." This phrase stands out as the only mention in this letter of His coming again, but it would be taken up once more in Paul's last letter (see II Tim. 4:8). It is also remarkable that this letter always refers to Christ Jesus, in that order, except in one verse in which the order is Jesus Christ (1:16) and two verses in this chapter which give His names in full: Our Lord, even Jesus, who is the Christ (6:3, 14).

Paul's next words are a doxology filled with grandeur: "which in its own times he shall shew, who is the blessed and only Potentate, the King of kings and Lord of lords" (6:15). The day of Christ's return is seen as a fixed time which still belongs to the future, but there is no doubt about the event itself. It will occur "in its own times," a phrase which would affirm the fact but leave the time indefinite (cf. 2:6). The Lord Jesus will manifest Himself by appearing (6:14) in due season; He will then be seen in all His glory. His true identity will be revealed as "the blessed and only potentate," a unique designation in biblical literature. Paul had applied the word *blessed* to God in one other verse when he spoke of "the gospel of the glory of the blessed God" (1:11); it was used to describe God as one whose experience is the absolute perfection of bliss. The word *potentate* is nowhere else employed with reference to God; it is qualified by the adjective *only* in a way that marks Him out as unique. He was invested with the princely splendor of a sovereign who is without peer or equal. Further He is "the King of kings and Lord of lords," an oriental superlative in common use in Persia. There was an Old Testament precedent in the words of Moses: "The LORD your God, he is God of gods, and Lord of lords" (Deut. 10:17; cf. Ps. 136:2–3; Dan. 2:47). But Paul's exact phrase was caught up in the account of the apocalyptic vision of John the Divine: "He hath on his garment and on his thigh a name written, KING OF KINGS, AND LORD OF LORDS" (Rev. 19:16; cf. 17:14). So this twofold title must have been one of the earliest ascriptions applied to Christ as the King of Glory and the Lord of all.

But this did not exhaust what Paul meant to convey; he had yet to complete the titles by giving their implications: "who only hath immortality, dwelling in light unapproachable; whom no man hath seen, nor can see: to whom be honour and power eternal. Amen" (6:16). The concept of immortality is meant to lift our eyes beyond the sphere of time to an endless life in glory. The expression is qualified in this verse through his use of the word *only:* "Who only hath immortality." God alone has immortality as an inherent attribute, for He alone is the author of life. But it is His will to impart this gift to His people in the day of resurrection when "this mortal must put on immortality" (I Cor. 15:53). But Paul had more to add; his mind was still absorbed in thought's ascent. God dwells in a sphere of light to which no man can approach; no man has seen or can see Him face to face in glory. The background for this statement was the experience of Moses whose fervent longing had been that God would show him His glory. But that was not to be; he had heard the divine response: "Thou canst not see my face: for man shall not see me and live" (Exod. 33:20). God hid Moses in a cleft of the

rock when He passed by so that Moses saw a trailing cloud
of glory. God clothes Himself with light as with a garment
(Ps. 104:2); who can stand before such dazzling splendor?[3]
His majesty and holiness make up that robe of light; man can
only bow in awe and wonder in His presence. To Him must
be ascribed honor and power eternal; the choice of terms is
linked with the earlier use of the word *potentate* (6:15). On
that magnificent chord the doxology comes to an end. *Amen.*

3. Ibid., p. 90.

"Paul, a servant of God and an apostle of Jesus Christ, . . . to Titus, my true child after a common faith."

Titus 1:1–4

No less than nine of the Pauline letters were addressed to a particular church or congregation. Only four were written to a single person: one to Philemon, two to Timothy, one to Titus. The letter to Titus was closely related in spirit and content to the First Epistle to Timothy. Many verbal resemblances as well as its overall directions suggest that it belongs to the same phase in Paul's life and circumstances. The salutation was longer and more formal than in the Epistle to Timothy. This was not because Paul held Titus in less esteem; it was rather because of the official character of its contents and the absence of the personal injunctions addressed to Timothy. Paul wrote to Titus as a trusted colleague, but it was the church in Crete that he had in mind. There is nothing to say how or when or by whom that church was planted. Crete had been part of a Roman province for upward of a hundred years. Jewish emigrants had become a settled community on the island for a still longer period. There were Cretans, either Jews or proselytes, at Jerusalem on the day of Pentecost (Acts 2:11), but the only reference to Crete in connection with Paul was on his voyage under military escort to Rome. The ship in which he sailed passed "under the lee of Crete" and berthed at Fair Havens (Acts 27:7–8). Paul wanted to winter at Fair Havens, but the master

of the vessel pressed on toward Phoenix. The ship was caught
in a storm that swept it on to wreckage on the rocks of Malta.
But it seems that Paul had subsequently been to Crete with
Titus and had observed features of life on the island which
were deplorable. Titus had been left there or sent back to
straighten things out where the infant church was concerned, and this letter was written for his guidance and
encouragement.

The letter begins with a salutation in which Paul presents
his credentials in case any Cretan were to inquire by what
authority he wrote: "Paul, a servant of God, and an apostle of
Jesus Christ, according to the faith of God's elect, and the
knowledge of the truth which is according to godliness" (1:1).
The word *servant* is not as strong as the word *slave*, but it
marked Paul out as a bondservant of God. Nowhere else did
he write about himself as a servant of God, though two of his
letters began with his designation as a servant of Jesus Christ
(Rom. 1:1; Phil. 1:1). Paul had also proclaimed himself to the
church at Corinth as "your servant for Jesus' sake" (II Cor.
4:5). But the servant of God was as well an apostle of Jesus
Christ: one who had seen the Lord, even though it was as
"one born out of due time" (I Cor. 15:8). Paul had not been
present when the Twelve were called, but the Lord had
appeared to Paul and had called him just as surely as if he
had been one of that group which stood on the hills overlooking the Sea of Galilee. He may have been the last as well
as the least of all the apostles, yet by the grace of God he was
in no respect behind the first or the chief of all the apostles
(see I Cor. 15:9; II Cor. 12:11). This was all in accord with "the
faith of God's elect;" they were ready to bear witness to the
truth of Paul's claim. This phrase which speaks of God's
people as God's elect occurs in two other Pauline verses
(Rom. 8:33; Col. 3:12); in each case it lends an impressive
emphasis to the idea of God's choice of those who were His
people. The faith of God's elect was linked with the knowledge of the truth which was according to godliness. This is

comparable with what he wrote about "the doctrine which is according to godliness" (I Tim. 6:3). Knowledge of truth and sound doctrine would be nothing unless in harmony with godliness.

But this apostleship was not bound by the circumstances of that particular moment; it was oriented toward a goal fixed in eternity: "in hope of eternal life, which God, who cannot lie, promised before times eternal" (1:2). There is an interesting variation of this theme in the corresponding salutation of Paul's final letter: "Paul, an apostle of Christ Jesus by the will of God, according to the promise of the life which is in Christ Jesus" (II Tim. 1:1). The "hope of life" in this verse takes the place of "the promise of life" in the latter context. The phrase *in hope* was used by Paul when he stood before Festus and Agrippa and spoke in self-defense: "And now I stand here to be judged for the hope of the promise made of God unto our fathers" (Acts 26:6).[1] That hope was the basis on which Paul's whole life of dedicated service had been founded, and that promise drew all its strength from the fact that it came from God who cannot lie. It seems strange to learn that this great Scriptural axiom was first voiced by Balaam: "God is not man that he should lie; Neither the son of man that he should repent" (Num. 23:19; cf. I Sam. 15:29; Heb. 6:18). The phrase *"that cannot lie"* is the translation of an adjective which means free from falsehood. The full moral force of that word is felt in this context in its confirmation of the absolute certainty of the promise of God. That promise was given before times eternal; before the world began. The same phrase was used to speak of ". . . his own purpose and grace, which was given us in Christ Jesus before times eternal" (II Tim. 1:9). The long-sounding echo of an eternity before the world began and an eternity that will stretch far beyond this world rings through the words: "eternal life . . . times eternal."

Nevertheless there is a plain contrast between the times

---

1. The same preposition is used in both phrases in the original Greek.

eternal and times temporal: "but in his own seasons manifested his word in the message, wherewith I was intrusted
according to the commandment of God our Saviour" (1:3).
This new phrase, *"in his own seasons,"* was employed before
in the Greek text of the First Epistle to Timothy (see I Tim.
2:6; 6:15). But in this verse, the word *seasons* was in contrast
with the word *times* (cf. 1:2): it points to the appropriate
moment, while the latter refers to the duration or the succession of time.[2] That great promise, given before the world
began, was fulfilled through the revelation of God who was
"in Christ reconciling the world unto himself" (II Cor. 5:19).
This was His Word for all mankind: and it was this message
with which Paul had been put in trust. He could hardly so
much as make mention of that message without a fresh
recollection of his role as trustee. Paul's use of the personal
pronoun was most emphatic: "wherewith I was intrusted."
This ought to be compared with his statements elsewhere in
these letters: he had spoken freely of "the gospel of the glory
of the blessed God, which was committed to my trust" (I Tim.
1:11; cf. II Tim. 1:11). He was always vividly sensitive to one
great fact in his experience of the mercies of God: that was
the fact that the Evangel had been intrusted to him. Nor was
that a claim which he would venture to make apart from his
amazing assurance of its heavenly origin: it was "according
to the commandment of God our Saviour." The whole phrase
was identical with an earlier utterance (I Tim. 1:1), and twice
more in the course of this letter he would speak of God our
Savior (Titus 2:10; 3:4). It was on this lofty level that his eyes
came to rest before he went on to address Titus as the recipient of this letter.

So Paul named the trusted colleague to whom he was
writing: "to Titus, my true child after a common faith" (1:4). It
is remarkable that the name of Titus, like that of Luke, never
appears in the Book of Acts and yet Titus's name was intimately linked with that of Paul in apostolic labors. Titus is

2. Guthrie, *Pastoral Epistles*, p. 182.

first mentioned at the time of the Gentile controversy when he accompanied Paul and Barnabas to Jerusalem (Gal. 2:1). Titus was a Gentile convert who had not been through the rite of circumcision; this made him a test case in the controversy. Paul refused to allow Titus to submit to the rite of circumcision lest that should be taken as a sign that the grace of God was not enough (see Gal. 2:3). Titus must have become one of Paul's more regular companions until Titus was chosen for a very difficult ministry at a time of crisis in the church of Corinth. It is clear that he was a man whose tact and skill endowed him with qualities of true leadership. Titus had carried a letter from Paul which was written with much anguish of heart and which has now been lost (II Cor. 2:4). Paul could not rest until Titus met him in Macedonia and brought him news that was of great comfort (II Cor. 2:13). Titus himself was full of joy, for his spirit had been refreshed by the change that had been wrought in the church (II Cor. 7:13). Titus then returned to Corinth with a further letter and was to spend some twelve months there while he organized the collection on behalf of the persecuted church in Jerusalem. Paul was glad to commend him in terms of high praise: "He is my partner and my fellow-worker to you-ward" (II Cor. 8:23). Titus dropped out of sight at that point and did not emerge again until this letter was written; but he must have gone with Paul to Crete after Paul's release from prison in Rome, and there he had remained in a situation that would demand all his gifts of wisdom and strength.

And Paul wrote to Titus in the affectionate language that was prompted by his tenderhearted concern: "Grace and peace from God the Father and Christ Jesus our Saviour" (1:4). Titus was addressed with an endearing expression exactly as Timothy had been: "my true child;" my own son (I Tim. 1:2). But there is a minor variation in the phrase that follows: "after a common faith." Does this reflect the idea that Titus was more robust as a son in the faith? It seems to link him more widely with all who had "obtained a like

69

precious faith" (II Peter 1:1) in "God our Saviour" (1:3). There is also one marked variation in the words of greeting compared with the parallel words in the two letters to Timothy. There it was "grace, mercy, peace" (I Tim. 1:2; II Tim. 1:2). But here mercy was left out and it was simply "grace and peace" as in all Paul's other letters. Such a greeting was a combination of a Greek and Hebrew form of salutation: grace was the Greek word of greeting, while peace was the Hebrew. This word of grace recalls God's most loving favor, totally undeserved, freely bestowed, never failing, always equal to all our need. The word of peace speaks of harmonious relationship, rich in meaning on the human level, infinitely more so on the level where God Himself belongs. There was nothing merely formal in such words of greeting from the veteran apostle; they would stir up all that Titus had come to know of the loving-kindness of God. That grace and peace were said to flow from "God the Father and Christ Jesus our Saviour." In the Timothy Epistles, Paul spoke of Christ Jesus our Lord (I Tim. 1:2; II Tim. 1:2); the change to Christ Jesus our Savior was small, but significant. The expression "God our Saviour" (1:3) had now become "Christ Jesus our Saviour" (1:4; cf. 2:13; 3:6); salvation was ascribed to the Father and to the Son (see Rev. 7:10).

11

*"For the grace of God hath appeared,
bringing salvation to all men."*
Titus 2:11-15

Titus was purposely left in Crete so that he could set in order "the things that were wanting" and could appoint elders for the congregation (1:5). Paul pointed out what were the essential characteristics of those whom Titus might choose for this office: they had to be blameless at home and in the church, hospitable, dedicated, and well-versed in apostolic teaching (1:6–9). Then Paul turned to those who were false teachers: they were unruly, frivolous, self-deceived; they were to be muzzled in order to prevent further damage. Paul could not be accused of an unjust judgment since his comments were all confirmed by a well-known Cretan philosopher who described his fellow Cretans as "always liars, evil beasts, idle gluttons" (1:12). Paul knew that this was true; such men deserved severe rebuke. Nothing could be worse than to find men who professed to know God, yet denied Him by the kind of life they led (1:10–16). Titus on the other hand was to teach only what became sound doctrine (2:1). He should address himself first to older men and women in order to insure that their manner of life was such as to commend what they held dear (2:2–5). Young men stood in need of sober-minded poise and control. Titus should prove himself as a pattern for them in sound doctrine, and that would then issue in word and deed that were beyond reproach (2:6–8). Servants, or slaves, were called on to act with honesty and courtesy "that they may adorn the doctrine of God our Saviour in all things"

(2:9–10). All these practical injunctions were then brought to a head with an appeal to the eternal verities of the gospel (2:11–15).

Paul found that he could not refer to "the doctrine of God our Saviour" without going on to enlarge on that subject: "For," he wrote, "the grace of God hath appeared, bringing salvation to all men" (2:11). The connecting particle *for* shows the movement of thought from God our Savior to the salvation that is for all. But the primary emphasis in this passage was on the grace of God: this was the strength and the keynote of all Pauline theology. He would return to this theme in the next chapter: "That, being justified by his grace, we might be made heirs according to the hope of eternal life" (3:7). There is nothing that man can do to purge his sense of guilt or to cleanse his soul from the stain of sin. Unless God reaches down to the place where man has sunk and lifts him up from the pit and the clay, he is lost beyond any hope of reclamation. But that is just what God has done; He sent His Son into the world to save men from their sins. That is an act of grace that flows from love so rich and free that it knows no measure: "for by grace have ye been saved through faith; and that not of yourselves: it is the gift of God" (Eph. 2:8). That grace appeared when "the kindness of God our Saviour, and his love toward man, appeared" (3:4). This word occurs only in two other verses (Luke 1:79; Acts 27:20); it means to shine on. The grace of God shone forth in the fulness of time, bringing salvation, or deliverance, to all men (see I Tim. 2:4). That magnificent and universal concept of the saving efficacy of grace reaches out to people of all classes: the old, the young, the slave, and even the Cretan.

The grace of God is seen almost as a personal instrument for the cultivation of a godly manner of life: "instructing us, to the intent that, denying ungodliness and worldly lusts, we should live soberly and righteously and godly in this present world" (2:12). It was ever vital to impress the ethic of serious character and godly conduct on those who were recent converts from idolatry and hedonism. The first element in that instruction was to teach the necessity for a twofold renunciation. They were to turn their back on all ungodliness, or impiety, the exact reverse of the godliness to which he had so often called Timothy's attention (I Tim. 2:2; 4:7, 8; 6:3, 5, 6, 11). They were also to renounce all worldly lusts, or desires, that were centered in a social system that was hostile to God. The word *lust* or desire need not have a moral connotation at all, but the context nearly always imparts to it a strong sense of stigma. That is assuredly the case in this verse where the word *worldly* reflects the view that the love of the world must be inimical to love for God (see James 4:4; I John 2:15). But this instruction was not confined to the negative aspects of life. Converts were to turn their back on one set of values so that they could turn their eyes to a fresh set of ideals. They were called to live in a way that would please God. To live soberly would be to prove themselves soberminded, just as Paul had called for in the case of elders, and the aged, and the young (1:8; 2:2, 5, 6). To live righteously was the pattern of life which he himself had sought to set before others (I Thess. 2:10). To live godly was the exact antithesis of the ungodliness they were called to renounce. "Yea," he would write, "and all that would live godly in Christ Jesus shall suffer persecution" (II Tim. 3:12).

Paul ended the last verse on the note of this present world, the age to which they belonged; but he at once went on to point to the future when the Lord would return to reign as King: "looking for the blessed hope and appearing of the glory of our great God and Saviour Jesus Christ" (2:13). There is a similar saying in an earlier epistle in which a compound of the same verb appears: "waiting for the revelation of our Lord Jesus Christ" (I Cor. 1:7). The grace of God in their hearts would teach them to look for the blessed hope and glorious appearing of one who is both God and Christ. This hope was not just an empty shadow, with no substance and no reality; it was based on a sure prospect and was rich in blessing. It was more than hope of eternal life (1:2), because it was centered on the person of Christ in His glory. The word *appearing* is a cognate of the verb he had just employed (2:11), and was used no less than four times in the Timothy Epistles (I Tim. 6:14; II Tim. 1:10; 4:1, 8). He would shine forth in that resplendent majesty which can belong only to the Godhead, and hence He is fitly described as our great God and Savior Jesus Christ. This most striking declaration of the absolute deity of Christ is a unique statement in the language employed. Nowhere was the word *great* applied to God when God alone was being spoken of; His greatness was always assumed. But that word was wholly appropriate in a phrase in which Christ was identified as God. This short letter in each chapter speaks first of God our Savior (1:3; 2:10; 3:4), and then of Christ our Savior (1:4; 2:13; 3:6). But this is the verse that supplies the most splendid tribute to the equality of Christ with the Father.

Perhaps it was Paul's use of that special designation "Saviour" as he spoke of Christ that led to a larger statement about His saving work on our behalf: "who gave himself for us, that he might redeem us from all iniquity, and purify unto himself a people for his own possession, zealous of good works" (2:14). This verse begins with one of Paul's favorite expressions about the self-giving of Christ for the sake of others. He "gave himself for our sins that he might deliver us out of this present evil world" (Gal. 1:4); He "gave himself a ransom for all" (I Tim. 2:6). God so loved that He gave His Son; and the Son of God so loved that He gave Himself. He stood where we deserved to stand, and gave Himself on our behalf. This He did that He might redeem us from all iniquity. Paul had in mind the words of the psalmist: "he shall redeem Israel from all his iniquities" (Ps. 130:8). Christ's own self-offering was the ransom He had to pay in order to redeem those who had been the slaves of sin. He bought them with a price, and that price was His death on the cross. He did more than redeem them from bondage to all iniquity and so restore them to spiritual freedom; He also purified them, cleansed them, washed them white as snow, and made them a people for His own possession, "a peculiar treasure" (Exod. 19:5), chosen, special, loved and precious. Such a redeemed people ought to become zealous of good works, for such good works would be the proof of their redemption (3:8). The same practical conclusion marked the end of Paul's definitive statement on the doctrine of grace: "For we are his workmanship, created in Christ Jesus for good works, which God afore prepared that we should walk in them" (Eph. 2:10).

The whole passage ends with a personal injunction for Titus's encouragement: "These things speak and exhort and reprove with all authority. Let no man despise thee" (2:15). This verse looks back over all that Paul had written since the salutation and sums it up with his typical brevity in such matters. Titus would need to be mindful both of practical instructions and of doctrinal foundations. Perhaps Paul's last words would ring through his soul as he thought of good works. "Sin alone renders men contemptible; holiness alone honourable."[1] Therefore Titus was called to "declare these things" (RSV); in so doing, he was to exhort and reprove. He was to preach the word without fear or favor, whether in or out of season, and to "reprove, rebuke, exhort, with all long-suffering and teaching" (II Tim. 4:2). He would exhort those who stood in need of encouragement; he would reprove those who deserved censure. And he was to do this as one who had been armed with all authority. The word in the Greek text is found only in the Pauline letters, and it always occurs with the meaning of a divine command. Titus was to speak and act as one who was well aware of the authority vested in him as God's servant. It might have been thought that Paul would end this section with that telling sentence; but Paul went on to add one more throwaway expression: "Let no man despise thee." It reads like an afterthought, but

1. Simpson, *Pastoral Epistles*, p. 110.

was in fact very relevant. Paul did not speak about youthfulness as in the case of Timothy (see I Tim. 4:12); Titus was an older and more seasoned leader. But there might well be some who would try to make light of his authority; Paul warned him not to be afraid nor to succumb to that form of Cretan hostility.

12

"But when the kindness of God our Saviour, and his love toward man, appeared, not by works done in righteousness, which we did ourselves, but according to his mercy he saved us."

Titus 3:4-7

Paul was keenly aware of the need for honest conduct in the eyes of the local authorities in order to commend the gospel (see Rom. 13:1-7; I Tim. 2:1-2). It was vital that his converts should be known as worthy members of their community, and should not be confused with its dissident elements. Therefore Paul told Titus to put them in mind of civic duties: they were to be subject to rulers, to authorities, to be obedient, and to respond to the call to every good work (3:1). Paul may have feared lest the Cretan spirit of trouble-making in political affairs should creep into the church. He would therefore have his converts prove their spiritual maturity by a proper respect for magistrates and officials. This would require them to avoid all censorious and provocative language, and to display both gentleness and courtesy toward all men (3:2). This is comparable with the criteria which Paul prescribed for a bishop who had to be without reproach: "no brawler, no striker; but gentle, not contentious" (I Tim. 3:3). Such words imply all too plainly what the Cretans were by nature; they were all too like the picture painted by their own revered philosopher (see 1:12). Nevertheless much the same could have been said of Paul and Titus before they knew the grace of God: "For we also were aforetime foolish, disobedient, deceived, serving divers lusts and pleasures, living in malice and envy, hateful, hating one another" (3:3; cf. I Cor. 6: 9–11; Eph. 4:17–24). Paul could not have described the Cretans more harshly; but he chose to speak from his own experience and to include Titus in his remarks. That is what we were like: what a backdrop for his next words about the grace of God!

Paul's heart invariably overflowed when he thought of what he had been and of what God had done for him: "But when the kindness of God our Saviour, and his love toward man, appeared" (3:4). What had once been the case was not the end of the story; the word *but* signals the great contrast which was brought about by the intervention of God Himself. That intervention began from the human standpoint at the moment when His kindness appeared; that is, when the grace of God shone forth (2:11). Perhaps this was meant to refer to the incarnation, for that was when the Son of God came into the world. Here Paul used an impersonal term in order to speak of the kindness of God in His plan to save us. No other New Testament writer employed this term, but Paul used it freely. Twice it referred to the kindness that ought to be discernible in men (II Cor. 6:6; Col. 3:12); elsewhere it spoke of the astonishing goodness of God. Sometimes indeed the word *goodness* is employed to translate this term (see Rom. 2:4; 11:22). But the noble meaning of this word is made clear in the Ephesian utterance: "that in the ages to come he might shew the exceeding riches of his grace in kindness toward us in Christ Jesus" (Eph. 2:7). But the kindness of God as our Savior was linked with his love toward man. The phrase *love toward man* translates one word in the Greek text. It was sometimes used of human kindness in cases of distress as in the case of the barbarians on the island of Malta who "shewed us no common kindness" (Acts 28:2). When it was used of God as in this verse, it meant His love for all mankind; and that love had appeared, shone forth in the midst of darkness, when His Son came into the world.

The main clause in this long section follows in words that lie at the very heart of Pauline theology: "not by works done in righteousness, which we did ourselves, but according to his mercy he saved us" (3:5). This clause may sound harsh and involved, but its meaning has a pellucid clarity. There is in all men a profound instinct that makes them strive after recognition in the presence of God by means of works done in righteousness. Paul had in mind those who tried to accrue merit by strict conformity to the law of Moses. That was what Paul had done; he had spared no effort to win divine favor. Countless thousands have worn themselves out on the same hopeless treadmill: self-denial, self-discipline, penitence, devotion: there is no end to the tale of human effort. But all to no avail, as Paul had found; it was not by works he had done that he was saved. Article IX of the Articles of Religion is decisive and emphatic in its language: "Man is very far gone from original righteousness, and is of his own nature inclined to evil." Augustus Toplady summed up the whole situation in his great hymn with a superb simplicity of thought and phrase:

> Not the labors of my hands
> Can fulfil Thy law's demands;
> Could my zeal no respite know,
> Could my tears for ever flow,
> All for sin could not atone.
> Thou must save, and thou alone.

Not by works; not by self-effort; not by my own merit: no, no, no! But according to His mercy He saved us. Not by human merit, but by divine mercy—let it stand in letters of gold—*He saved us.*

Apart from that mercy, there could be no forgiveness and no acceptance with God; but because of mercy, "he saved us, through the washing of regeneration and renewing of the Holy Ghost" (3:5). Each phrase in this clause has been the subject of much debate, but the plain sense of the language is

79

the best guide to its meaning. The washing must refer to washing by water, just as in a similar utterance about the church: "that he might sanctify it, having cleansed it by the washing of water with the word" (Eph. 5:26). But the washing in this clause is linked with regeneration rather than with the word. This term occurs only in one other verse in the New Testament when it had a cosmic significance: "in the regeneration when the Son of man shall sit on the throne of his glory" (Matt. 19:28). Here it refers to the spiritual rebirth which can take place only in the inmost region of our being. The word *renewing* also has a parallel usage which throws light on its meaning: "be ye transformed by the renewing of your mind" (Rom. 12:2). This is indeed the work of the Holy Spirit as the agent in the restoration of the divine image. The two parts of this clause should be considered together and their significance is seen in the words addressed to Nicodemus: "Verily, verily, I say unto thee, Except a man be born of water and of the Spirit, he cannot enter into the kingdom of God" (John 3:5). The absence of the definite article before the word *Spirit* suggests that this saying was in the form of that figure of speech known as hendiadys. First Jesus spoke of the symbol; then He spoke of the substance: the washing of water was the symbol for the rebirth of the Spirit. So Paul combined symbolic language with sober reality in order to present a single truth: the Son of God saved us by the washing of water as a symbol of regeneration and by the actual renewing of the Holy Spirit as the mighty agent in this new creation.

But this mention of the Holy Spirit at once led Paul to a larger statement on the subject: "which he poured out upon us richly through Jesus Christ our Saviour" (3:6). The same Holy Spirit who was instrumental in that new birth in the inmost region of the human spirit is the divine agent on whom alone we must rely for ongoing growth in holiness. But Paul used the aorist tense of the verb *poured out* so as to point to a historical landmark. It is reminiscent of the Pentecostal experience which was described in the same terms: "having received of the Father the promise of the Holy Ghost, he hath poured forth this, which ye see and hear" (Acts 2:33). But the primary reference in this context must be to the experience of those who were embraced by the word *us;* that is, Paul and Titus. God poured out this gift of the Holy Spirit in their lives with unreserved abandon. Paul used the word *richly* in order to describe the generous and abundant giving of God. He had employed the same word in a not dissimilar spirit before: "... God ... giveth us richly all things to enjoy" (I Tim. 6:17). And this gift is mediated through Christ as our Savior. He had taken His place at the right hand of God and received gifts for the church on earth; therefore He had poured out that gift of the Holy Spirit as richly and freely as it had been received. Once more, and for the third time, Paul wrote of Jesus Christ our Savior (cf. 1:4; 2:13) in a context which overflows with salvation as its main theme. It was when the kindness of God our Savior appeared that He saved us; and that saving work was fulfilled through Jesus Christ as our mighty Savior.

The grand purpose of God's saving work in man's soul is then proclaimed in the ever memorable language of that chief of sinners whom Christ came to save: "that, being justified by his grace, we might be made heirs according to the hope of eternal life" (3:7). The words *"being justified by his grace"* are almost in parenthesis, but they are of singular importance because they amplify or interpret the main clause: *he saved us* (3:5). We have been saved because we have been justified: pronounced not guilty; reckoned as righteous; acquitted before the bar of God; accepted in the presence of God. The Son of God took on Himself our sin; we have taken His righteousness. Such an exchange could be achieved only by grace; it is so far beyond all that man might dream or deserve that it would be unknown but for the grace of God. The whole phrase reads like an echo of the classical discussion on this subject: "Being justified freely by his grace through the redemption that is in Christ Jesus" (Rom. 3:24). There were similar expressions in two later verses in that letter: "Being therefore justified by faith" (Rom. 5:1); "being now justified by his blood" (Rom. 5:9). We are declared righteous as an act of grace, by means of faith, on the sole ground of the shed blood of Christ. Therefore He saved us so that we might become heirs according to the hope of eternal life. There was another paragraph in which Paul's line of thought moved from the basic need to be justified (Gal. 3:11) to the final issue of heirship (Gal. 3:29). This was also the case on a wider scale of development in the letter to the church at Rome. Those who had been "justified freely by his grace" (Rom. 3:24) were destined to become "heirs of God, and joint-heirs with Christ" (Rom. 8:17). So this passage concludes with the sure hope on which this heirship now rests; and that hope looks forward to its glorious fulfilment in eternal life (1:2).

13

> *"For God gave us not a spirit of fearfulness;*
> *but of power and love and discipline."*

II Timothy 1:3-7

Paul's long imprisonment in Rome apparently came to an end with his release after two years of being confined "in his own hired dwelling" (Acts 28:30). He then went back to Ephesus where in due course he left Timothy while he went on to the churches in Macedonia (I Tim. 1:3). This must have been followed by his visit to Crete where he had left Titus (Titus 1:5). Later he was to urge Titus to join him in Nicopolis where he planned to spend the winter (Titus 3:12). Then a veil of obscurity hides the course of events, though some details emerge from his final letter. Paul had been in Troas (II Tim. 4:13), and he had left Trophimus sick at Miletus (4:20). Then Paul was placed under arrest and his trial was transferred to the imperial city of Rome (1:17). It was from Rome that he wrote once more to Timothy, beginning with his customary salutation: "Paul, an apostle of Christ Jesus by the will of God, according to the promise of the life which is in Christ Jesus, to Timothy, my beloved child: Grace, mercy, peace, from God the Father and Christ Jesus our Lord" (1:1–2). It soon becomes clear that Paul was not only in prison (1:8), but also in chains (1:16). It was totally different from his own hired dwelling, for he had to suffer hardship as a malefactor (2:9). Paul had already made one appearance in court; it was a first preliminary examination. He had sent Crescens to Galatia, Titus to Dalmatia, Tychicus to Ephesus. Of his traveling companions, only Luke was with him. Paul longed to see

Timothy and urged him to come before winter; he would have Timothy bring Mark as well. The Lord who had preserved Paul from the mouth of the lion would indeed preserve him from all evil (4:17–18). But he knew that there was no escape from an adverse verdict which would result in a sentence of death. Therefore it was in the shadow of a violent martyrdom that Paul wrote this final letter, with its poignant emotions and its moving directions.

Paul's first words sprang from the personal memories that filled his mind and heart: "I thank God, whom I serve from my forefathers in a pure conscience, how unceasing is my remembrance of thee in my supplications" (1:3). The first expression, "I thank God," had been used before (I Tim. 1:12); it had a touch of style which was lacking in the general formula. But Paul could not lift up his heart to God without declaring his own position; he thought of God as one whom he strove to serve with a pure conscience. Paul had made the same claim in still stronger terms when he stood before the high priest years before: "I have lived before God in all good conscience until this day" (Acts 23:1). Paul did not speak in a boastful spirit, but in sober humility, for his aim was always to act in love "out of a pure heart and a good conscience" (I Tim. 1:5). Nor was that all, for he declared that his service for God could be traced back to his forebears. Paul would never allow anyone to despise or condemn the ancestry and traditions of those Hebrew fathers. To them had been given the covenants, the promises, and the oracles of God, and Paul rejoiced to recognize his unity with them in his service for God. But that clause was a semiprivate form of self-reference, and he returned to his main theme of thankfulness and remembrance. His words are not without an element of awkwardness: "I thank God . . . how unceasing is my remembrance of thee in my supplications." Paul could hardly have meant that he thanked God for his unceasing remembrance in prayer; it was rather that he would thank God as often as he remembered Timothy in prayer. Timothy as Paul's dear child was in his heart and in his prayers more than ever as the threat of death grew more real.

The intensity of feeling which lay beneath Paul's words could hardly be restrained: ". . . night and day longing to see thee, remembering thy tears, that I may be filled with joy" (1:3–4). The phrase "night and day" had been linked with prayers and supplications before (I Tim. 5:5), but the context in this case makes it more natural to link it with Paul's expression of longing to see Timothy. This would be all the more telling since Timothy was in Ephesus where for three years Paul had labored to warn "every one night and day with tears" (Acts 20:31). It is a phrase that brings out the seriousness of what was in Paul's heart, for morning and evening alike, as he prayed for Timothy, he was filled with nostalgic desire like that of a father yearning for his favorite son. The word *longing* was not new in Paul's vocabulary. He had told the church at Rome that he longed to see them though they had never met (Rom. 1:11). He had written with much stronger personal emotion to the church at Philippi: "God is my witness, how I long after you all in the tender mercies of Christ Jesus" (Phil. 1:8). The full force of this deep longing for Timothy may be judged by comparison with a kindred passage: "what thanksgiving can we render unto God for you, for all the joy wherewith we joy for your sakes before our God; night and day praying exceedingly that we may see your face?" (I Thess. 3:9–10). This longing was heightened because Paul remembered Timothy's tears at the time of their last farewell. Timothy's sensitive nature would make him all the more susceptible to that moment of sweet sorrow, and Paul could not forget those tears. But tears and joy are more nearly related than we may think. It is certain that tears made Paul long the more to see Timothy again so that they might be turned to joy. If Paul were to see Timothy again, their sorrow would vanish and their joy would be full (see John 16:22).

Memory was still at work, for news Paul had perhaps

recently received reminded him of Timothy in one special respect: "having been reminded of the unfeigned faith that is in thee; which dwelt first in thy grandmother Lois, and thy mother Eunice; and I am persuaded, in thee also" (1:5). Paul was deeply aware of the debt which he owed to his own forefathers, and that made him doubly sympathetic with the domestic piety with which Timothy had been surrounded. Paul was mindful of the unfeigned faith which Timothy possessed, and his possession of such a faith made up for the want of a more robust spirit in his other activities. Paul had spoken of faith unfeigned in his earlier epistle (I Tim. 1:5); faith that was pure, wholesome, undissembled, the kind of trust that would lodge in the heart of a true man of God. The thought of such a faith seems to have stimulated recollections of the two godly women, Lois and Eunice, Timothy's grandmother and mother. It was fifteen years or more since Paul had come to Lystra on his second journey and discovered Timothy, the son of a devout Jewess and a Gentile father (Acts 16:1). Timothy was like Augustine, with a godly mother and a pagan father. That faith of which Paul spoke dwelt first in Lois; perhaps through her it came to be shared by Eunice. They must have been eminent examples of those whose lives were ruled by faith that was pure and undissembled. Paul was convinced that the faith which dwelt in them dwelt in Timothy as well, for he had grown up in a home where from early childhood he was nurtured in the Scriptures. Perhaps grandmother and mother and son all owed their faith in Christ to Paul's apostolic witness; it affords a lovely picture of the homelife that nurtured three generations for God.

The rich variety in the succession of words about remembering came to a head in Paul's personal charge to Timothy: "For the which cause I put thee in remembrance that thou stir up the gift of God, which is in thee through the laying on of my hands" (1:6). It was for the sake of this faith that Paul sought to put Timothy in remembrance; Paul wanted to evoke the strong personal memory of an event and a gift that lay in the past. It was the same event and the same gift of which he spoke in the earlier epistle: "Neglect not the gift that is in thee, which was given thee by prophecy, with the laying on of the hands of the presbytery" (I Tim. 4:14). Paul's words were dynamic: neglect not; stir up. He wanted to kindle into flame the fire that once began to burn. There was no attempt to define the gift of God, but H. C. G. Moule calls it a grace-gift.[1] It was a gift of grace; it could come only as a result of God's loving favor. Further, that gift was said to be in Timothy; it was spiritual in quality and character, and it was linked with the laying on of Paul's hands and those of the elders. Paul's words had a historic occasion in mind and seem to speak of a rite of ordination. Perhaps it had been at Lystra, perhaps in Ephesus; Paul had solemnly laid his hands on Timothy and the elders had shared in that act of ordination. But the laying on of hands was no more than a symbolic expression of the luminous enduing of the Spirit which Paul longed to impart to Timothy. The gift of God belonged to Timothy's inner spiritual experience; it was meant to furnish him with grace and authority in the exercise of his ministry. Paul would therefore encourage Timothy to stir into flame the glowing embers of that grace-gift from God.

Paul's use of the connecting particle at the start of a new sentence shows that he had more to say about the gift of God: "For God gave us not a spirit of fearfulness; but of power and love and discipline" (1:7). This verse in some measure defines the gift of God: what it was not, as well as what it was. It was given to *us;* that is, to Paul as well as to Timothy, for Paul like Timothy had received the laying on of hands (Acts 13:3). It was not a spirit of fearfulness; it had nothing to do with an attitude of cowardice or diffidence. Was this a mild thrust at Timothy's natural lack of force and vigor? It is reminiscent of Paul's reassurance for those whom

1. H. C. G. Moule, *Studies in Second Timothy,* p. 46.

he called sons of God: "ye received not the spirit of bondage again unto fear; but ye received the spirit of adoption, whereby we cry Abba, Father" (Rom. 8:15). The words serve as "a foil" to the positive assertion of what they had received;[2] God gave them a spirit of power and love and discipline. The gift of power may not result in a dynamic ministry, but it imparts strength of purpose so that out of weakness men are made strong. "A man in Christ counts for more than a man by himself."[3] Many of God's servants who may have been timid when left to their natural resources have found a new source of courage when God has laid His hand on them. The gift of love was the essence of all faithful service for God, as it was the essence of His own self-giving service for men. And the gift of a sound mind (1:7, AV), or self-command, or discipline was equally essential for one called to guide and rule in the church of God. Such a spirit would cause him to act "with seemly reverence and restraint."[4] It was with these reassuring words that Paul sought to stimulate and encourage Timothy, his son in the faith.

2. Simpson, *Pastoral Epistles*, p. 123.
3. Ibid.
4. John R. W. Stott, *Guard the Gospel*, p. 31.

14

"Be not ashamed therefore of the testimony of our Lord, nor of me his prisoner: but suffer hardship with the gospel according to the power of God."

II Timothy 1:8-14

The text moved on from the several elements which contributed to molding Timothy's character to the gospel message which he had been called to proclaim. The word *therefore* marks the closeness in thought between this new section and what had been written: "Be not ashamed therefore of the testimony of our Lord, nor of me his prisoner: but suffer hardship with the gospel according to the power of God" (1:8). Paul learned from bitter experience the strength of that plausible temptation to feel ashamed. He won that battle, and his triumph was expressed in the ringing declaration: "I am not ashamed of the gospel: for it is the power of God unto salvation to every one that believeth" (Rom. 1:16). Therefore Paul could encourage Timothy not to allow any false sense of shame to cause him to shrink from testifying to Christ as Lord. He had used a similar expression in writing to Corinth: "even as the testimony of Christ was confirmed in you" (I Cor. 1:6). The word *testimony* is indeed broad enough to take in all aspects of the gospel witness to Christ: it would not be without shame or ignominy in the eyes of Jews and Gentiles who saw it as scandal or as moonshine. Equally, Timothy was not to be ashamed of Paul because of his imprisonment; it was for the Lord's sake (Eph. 3:1; Philem. 1, 9).

Many of Paul's former converts had deserted him because of the social stigma or the political danger of their friendship with a man on trial for his life: "This thou knowest, that all that are in Asia turned away from me" (1:15). Paul could not bear to think that it might be so in the case of Timothy; Timothy was called to suffering rather than shame. He was to take his share of ill-treatment and to suffer hardship with the gospel (cf. 2:3; 4:5).[1] And he would be fortified for this purpose "according to the power of God."

The line of thought moves from the broad mention of the gospel to its "central affirmation,"[2] namely, that *God saved us:* "who saved us, and called us with a holy calling, not according to our works, but according to his own purpose and grace, which was given us in Christ Jesus before times eternal" (1:9). Paul could never forget this great truth of divine grace and mercy: God had rescued him from total ruin when rescue seemed beyond human expectation. But that saving act of grace did not stand alone; it was coupled with the fact that He "called us with a holy calling." The call of God comes with the "tenderest magnetism" in order to decide our will and so incline us to respond.[3] "God is faithful, through whom ye were called into the fellowship of his Son Jesus Christ our Lord" (I Cor. 1:9). Here the emphasis is on that call as a holy calling; forgiveness leads to holiness when God saves us. That was "not according to our works, but according to his own purpose and grace." It was not due to any virtue or any merit in us; it was not a matter of desert or reward; there was nothing to attract His mercy; it was altogether an act of grace. Paul's words reiterate what he had told Titus: "not by works done in righteousness, which we did ourselves, but according to his mercy he saved us" (Titus 3:5). The emphasis for Timothy was placed on the sovereign character of God,

---

1. Guthrie, *Pastoral Epistles,* p. 128.
2. Stott, *Guard the Gospel,* p. 24.
3. Moule, *Studies in Second Timothy,* p. 51.

for His purpose and grace are the bedrock of salvation and vocation. The phrase *according to His purpose* is found elsewhere with a similar emphasis (see Rom. 8:28; Eph. 1:11); this verse links it with grace to give it a special significance in this context. And that was not a thing of the moment; it was "given us in Christ Jesus" from all eternity. The phrase *before times eternal* tries to convey what no words can express; the love of God for us was in full force "before the world began" (AV; cf. Titus 1:2).

But all that God planned in eternity came to actual fruition in the fulness of time: "but hath now been manifested by the appearing of our Saviour Christ Jesus, who abolished death, and brought life and incorruption to light through the gospel" (1:10). The grand purpose of God, hidden from the knowledge of the ages, was at last made manifest by the appearing of Christ as our Savior (Luke 2:11). Paul used the same word to point to the Second Advent (Titus 2:13); but there is no doubt that here he had the Incarnation in mind. Paul's use of the name and titles of Our Savior Christ Jesus was the spark that kindled his thought into the flame of a fresh and "glowing parenthesis."[4] Paul had recourse to the aorist tense for the verbs because, though still in the future, he viewed these things as a finished reality. What did Christ do as our Savior? He abolished death, annulled it, disarmed it, so that it has now lost its sting. Paul used the same verb in the future tense when he wrote of the consummation of all things that is yet to come: "The last enemy that shall be abolished is death" (I Cor. 15:26). Christ met death in His own person so that He might rescue those ". . . who through fear of death were all their lifetime subject to bondage" (Heb. 2:15). Nor was that all: He brought life and immortality to light (1:10, AV; RSV). The word *life* is enhanced by the further word *immortality:* it was life that knows no corruption, will not diminish, cannot decay. This had been brought to light through the gospel. It

4. Simpson, *Pastoral Epistles*, p. 125.

was more or less obscured in the half-light of the Old Testament, but has now been fully disclosed through the good news of Christ's death and resurrection. What if Paul were soon to hear himself sentenced to death? He would lift up his heart with a ringing shout of triumph: Christ has abolished death; He has brought life and immortality to light!

Paul could not mention the gospel and its central message without also mentioning his appointed ministry: "Whereunto I was appointed a preacher, and an apostle, and a teacher. For the which cause I suffer also these things: yet I am not ashamed" (1:11–12). This echoed the claim made in his earlier epistle: "whereunto I was appointed a preacher and an apostle (I speak the truth, I lie not), a teacher of the gentiles in faith and truth" (I Tim. 2:7). Paul did not now repeat the strong claim to veracity, neither did he refer again to the gentiles. But in each case, he made his point with an emphatic personal pronoun; it would help to express his own sense of profound wonder.[5] Paul had not chosen himself for this task; it was a ministry to which he had been appointed, and he named the same three categories as before. As a preacher, he was like a herald with a message to proclaim; as an apostle, he was like one of the Twelve and a witness to the Resurrection; as a teacher, he was like one of the scribes who had to impart the truth. Paul had been called to do or be many other things as well, but it was because of his dedication to this threefold calling that he was now in chains. This is made clear by the phrase which he had employed before: "for the which cause" (1:6). He had already summoned Timothy not to be ashamed of the gospel, but to take his share of whatever suffering it might entail (1:8). Now Paul spoke of his own experience in each respect, although the order is reversed. He did not mince words as to his situation: "I suffer these things"; imprisonment, bonds, loneliness, the prospect of death. He was now called to a suffering ministry, but he was

5. Guthrie, *Pastoral Epistles*, p. 73.

not subdued. His voice rang out again with a note of triumph: yet I am not ashamed.

This led Paul to voice one of his greatest declarations of unshaken confidence in the Lord whose he was and whom he served: "for I know him whom I have believed, and I am persuaded that he is able to guard that which I have committed unto him against that day" (1:12). The ground on which Paul took his stand was his profound personal commitment to the Lord Jesus: For I know him whom I have believed. He cast the verbs in the perfect tense to mark the ongoing character of that experience: I knew, and I still know; I believed, and I still believe. Paul voiced his highest aspiration in this very spirit: "that I may know him" (Phil. 3:10). Paul longed to know Christ in His resurrection power and His sacrificial love, so that he might become conformable to His death and attain to His resurrection. It was because Paul knew Christ that he put his whole trust in Him with a simplicity and a totality of faith in all circumstances and all that the future might hold. Therefore he could go on to say: I am persuaded (1:5); he was convinced with a sense of finality that the Lord was able to guard, to hold in safe keeping, what was now in His hands. The phrase *that which I have committed* is paraphrastic; it may be more strictly rendered as "my deposit." Paul had something in mind, but the precise meaning of the word is indefinite. Was it another personal allusion? Did Paul mean that he had given himself, his life, his all, into the hands of one who would never cease to hold him secure? Perhaps; but the same word occurs in two other verses in which it can refer only to the gospel about which Paul had been speaking (I Tim. 6:20; II Tim. 1:14; cf. 1:10). God had entrusted Paul with the gospel; God would guard it against that day when He will come again in power and great glory. "The Person is not named; the Deposit is not described; the Day is not specified":[6] but the verse is a most telling declaration of faith.

6. Moule, *Studies in Second Timothy,* p. 57.

Paul's great testimony was a parenthesis at the heart of his main subject, and he turned back once more to his words of encouragement for Timothy: "Hold the pattern of sound words which thou hast heard from me, in faith and love which is in Christ Jesus. That good thing which was committed unto thee guard through the Holy Ghost which dwelleth in us" (1:13–14). The fact that Timothy was called to share in a suffering ministry (1:8) made it imperative that he should hold, or hold fast, that full apostolic doctrine he had received from Paul. Timothy could hardly miss the close link between the pattern of sound words and all that he had heard from Paul himself. The word *pattern* suggests an outline or standard (see I Tim. 1:16); it would remind Timothy of the sound words or wholesome teaching he had heard so often. This was to be his "guide or rule"; he was not to depart from it.[7] But it was not enough to hold to a dry and orthodox position; Timothy would need to illuminate it in faith and love which found their center in Christ Jesus. Paul then amplified this charge with emphasis on the character of that deposit and Timothy's duty to act as an effective guardian. The same phrase was employed, but the trust was transferred as it were from the Lord to Timothy as the Lord's servant: it was "that good thing which was committed unto thee." It was like a priceless treasure placed in Timothy's care; he was responsible to keep it safe. This was in fact a firm echo of the closing appeal in the earlier epistle: "O Timothy," Paul had written, "guard that which is committed unto thee" (I Tim. 6:20). Timothy was to guard it with unflagging vigilance, knowing that all around him in Asia men were falling away from the gospel (1:15). Nor would he be required to fulfil this duty in his strength alone; he could rely on "the Holy Ghost which dwelleth in us." It was as though a veteran warrior had passed his sword to a younger comrade-in-arms.

7. Stott, *Guard the Gospel,* p. 44.

15

"Thou therefore, my child, be strengthened in the grace that is in Christ Jesus."

II Timothy 2:1-2

There is exceeding tenderness in Paul's farewell words of encouragement for Timothy throughout this epistle. Paul knew that he could not escape from the certain prospect of an early sentence of death. He knew that great sorrow as a result was imminent for Timothy. Paul foresaw that Timothy, too, might soon be called to tread that hard road to martyrdom. And Paul longed to support Timothy in advance since Paul would no longer stand at Timothy's side or share in his ordeal. This longing was heightened in view of the desertion by many in Asia, and in particular, the defection of Phygelus and Hermogenes (1:15). Perhaps they were singled out and mentioned by name because they were the main cause of the trouble. But there was a shining contrast between their conduct and the splendid example of Onesiphorus. Paul could recall his name only with a renewed sense of gratitude and affection: "for he oft refreshed me, and was not ashamed of my chain" (1:16). Onesiphorus had been in Rome and had gone to endless trouble to track down Paul in his prison quarters. He had visited Paul, not once, nor twice, but often, to brace and cheer him with warm and friendly concern. Paul could repay him only with prayer for him and his house, but Paul reminded Timothy that this kindness in Rome was a continuance of his many acts of friendship before: "in how many things he ministered at Ephesus, thou knowest very well" (1:18). It was in view of this background that Paul addressed himself to Timothy with earnestness and affection, calling him to seek strength as he now stood on the threshold of an unknown future.

Paul chose words which would ring in Timothy's memory for years to come: "Thou therefore, my child, be strengthened in the grace that is in Christ Jesus" (2:1). Paul's use of the personal pronoun *thou* as an emphatic vocative would strike an impressive chord at the beginning. Failure on the part of many and the contrasting steadfast courage of Onesiphorus threw great weight on this word, linked as it was with the causal adverb: *thou therefore*. Paul knew well Timothy's natural diffidence; Timothy was sensitive, hesitant, and shy. Paul was deeply aware of the fears and the trials that would beset such a spirit. So then, in view of all these things, Timothy must "be strong" (AV), seek strength, strengthen himself. The verb was cast either in the simple passive or in the middle voice. J. R. W. Stott treats it as the former;[1] H. C. G. Moule takes it as the latter.[2] The same verb in the same mood and tense is found in a similar passage: "Finally, be strong in the Lord, and in the strength of his might" (Eph. 6:10). Paul summoned Timothy to deal with his anxieties, to seek strength or strengthen himself in the grace that is found in Christ Jesus. Timothy was to say to his nervous spirit what the psalmist had said: "Why art thou cast down, O my soul? And why art thou disquieted within me?" (Ps. 42:5). Such an appeal speaks to the hearts of all God's servants who may shrink from difficulty in loneliness and leadership. So Joshua was exhorted: "Be strong and of a good courage; . . . for the LORD thy God is with thee whithersoever thou goest" (Josh. 1:9). So Daniel was encouraged: "O man greatly beloved, fear not: peace be unto thee, be strong, yea, be strong" (Dan. 10:19).

Paul's words, spoken as to a child, pointed Timothy to the

1. Stott, *Guard the Gospel,* p. 49, footnote.
2. Moule, *Studies in Second Timothy,* p. 70.

source of all true strength with an unerring directness: "Thou therefore, my child, be strengthened in the grace that is in Christ Jesus." Timothy had to wear Paul's mantle of influence and leadership in the very province where Paul's authority had been basely disowned. Timothy would need all the strength he could command if he were to stand fast and hold his ground. But how could he summon strength to his aid? How could a man strengthen himself if he were all weakness? Are not all men nothing more than "frail children of dust, and feeble as frail"? What would such a reflex action achieve, if the middle voice be correct, except expose all his weakness? Would it not show up all the more clearly the inability and self-paralysis of an over-timid nature? No, Timothy was to look to the Christ who dwelt in his heart by faith; he would strengthen himself by a positive reliance on the grace found only in Christ. The New English Bible has an amplified translation of Paul's exhortation which is very helpful: "Take strength from the grace of God which is ours in Christ Jesus." The grace of God was a prime theme in these letters, and these words link that grace surely and firmly with the person of Christ. This is grace in its most simple application; it is the help that comes from God for those who have no power to help themselves. The grace of God which is ours by virtue of our union with Christ Jesus speaks of His presence in our lives and His action on our behalf. So the prophet of old boldly declared: to them that have no might, he will make his strength increase (Isa. 40:29). So Paul could pray for the faltering believer: "that he would grant you, according to the riches of his glory, that ye may be strengthened with power through his Spirit in the inward man" (Eph. 3:16).

Paul at once went on to indicate the tasks for which Timothy would need to seek that strength in Christ Jesus: "And the things which thou hast heard from me among many witnesses, the same commit thou to faithful men, who shall be able to teach others also" (2:2). This verse takes up the theme of Paul's earlier injunction to Timothy for unflinching adherence to sound doctrine: "Hold the pattern of sound words which thou hast heard from me, in faith and love which is in Christ Jesus" (1:13). Timothy received from Paul only that which Paul had received from Christ Himself. Paul did not owe his own understanding of truth to an apostolic mentor; he derived it direct through revelation of Christ (Gal. 1:12). And what he had received, he had in turn sought to impart to his child in the faith. The use of the same phrase is striking: "which thou hast heard from me." The fact that the verb is in the aorist tense seems to point to the totality of Paul's teaching across the years.[3] There was nothing hidden or private or secret about these things; it was not in the least like the gnostic teaching that truth had been reserved only for a spiritual elite. It was as far from that teaching as light is from darkness; Paul had taught Timothy in the presence of many witnesses. It is impossible to know who were in mind, or even whether these witnesses were confined to a single locality. Were they members of the congregation at Lystra (Acts 16:2)? Were they elders in the presbytery at Ephesus (I Tim. 4:14)? But that hardly matters. Timothy had served as an apprentice in the gospel with Paul since Paul's second missionary journey, and it was well-known that he had heard from Paul all that he then sought to teach.

But the pattern of sound doctrine which he had heard from Paul was like a trust for which he was responsible for the sake of others: "The same commit thou to faithful men, who shall be able to teach others also." Paul was ready to finish the sentence about the things in which Timothy had been instructed, but Paul summed up what he had just written by his use of the phrase "the same." That was for the sake of clarity and emphasis; it would keep the object of the sentence in view. He chose a verb which would call to Timothy's remembrance the charge voiced in the earlier epistle: "This charge I commit unto thee, my child Timothy,

3. Stott, *Guard the Gospel*, p. 50.

according to the prophecies which went before on thee" (I Tim. 1:18). Paul had long since committed, entrusted, the elders of Lystra and of Ephesus to the Lord's keeping (Acts 14:23; 20:32). So now Timothy was exhorted to commit the things which he had heard as a sacred trust to men whom he judged to be faithful. There was still a remnant in those parts of Asia who adhered to the gospel in spite of the prevailing defection. But the fact that many had turned away made it all the more imperative for Timothy to exercise care and insight. The men whom he chose would become heirs and trustees of the apostolic truth and teaching. Therefore they were to be faithful; they were to be able to teach others. Integrity of character and ability for ministry were to be their hallmarks. Paul was concerned for the future; he was looking beyond his own imminent martyrdom, beyond Timothy's probable life span; he had other generations in mind. There-fore the things Paul had received were now entrusted to Timothy, while Timothy in turn was charged to choose faithful men as trustees for the future.

So Paul wrote to Timothy out of the wealth of his own experience: "Thou therefore, my child, be strengthened in the grace that is in Christ Jesus." Paul wrote to Timothy as a father might write, and he used that endearing expression, "my child," with a mingling of affection and authority (see I Tim. 1:2; 1:18; II Tim. 1:2). Paul knew well what it was to stand in need of strength, for there had been times when all his own strength had turned into weakness. He knew what it was to falter; he had felt as weak as a worm. It was almost as though his trials had been too great to bear, and he had cried out in anguish. But it was then, when things were at their worst, that Paul heard the voice of Jesus say: My grace is enough for you; it is equal to all your need (II Cor. 12:9). He had wondered at times if he could see things through; but he had found strength for his soul in that promise, and that strength had been made perfect in Paul's weakness. This nerved him with an invincible courage so that in a former imprisonment he boldly declared: "I have strength for all things through him who always makes me able" (cf. Phil. 4:13). That strength was not his own; it was not as though he could call on latent reserves to meet special demands. It was only his by virtue of his union with Christ; it was in Christ alone that he was strong for all things. The "all things" were limited and practical; not fanciful or infinite; not things that Paul would have chosen, but that God chose for him. David Livingstone out in darkest Africa had grasped this fact, and his passionate conviction still rings through his Journal: "If He be with me, I can do anything, anything, anything!" So Timothy would listen to the voice of the veteran apostle on the eve of martyrdom: "Thou therefore, my child, be strong, seek strength, strengthen thyself in the grace that is in Christ Jesus."

16

"Consider what I say; for the Lord shall give thee understanding in all things."

II Timothy 2:7-13

Paul followed up his words of encouragement with a call to "Suffer hardship with me, as a good soldier of Christ Jesus" (2:3). This was at once enforced by the comment that no soldier while on active duty can afford to become caught up in the trammels of the normal affairs of life. His one object must be to "please him who enrolled him as a soldier" (2:4). Then Paul employed another metaphor and spoke of the athlete who could not hope to win and wear the crown unless he observed the rules. This led to yet another metaphor; he spoke of the farmer who works hard in the field so that he may reap the harvest (2:5-6). These were his favorite metaphors, drawn from observation of the world through which he traveled. They all appeared elsewhere in his writings, and in particular, in these letters. They paved the way for a further exhortation in this context: it stands alone as a sentence which may look back or look forward. It illuminates Paul's understanding of his apostleship and his relationship to Timothy: "Consider what I say; for the Lord shall give thee understanding in all things" (2:7). Paul would have Timothy reflect on, or think over, what he had said or would yet say. But this was much more than ordinary counsel; it was advice given with "self-conscious apostolic authority."[1] The Lord Himself would grant understanding, perception or

1. Stott, *Guard the Gospel,* p. 59.

discernment, in the truth of these things. Nowhere else did Paul so definitely claim to be the bearer of God's message; here Paul declared that the Lord Himself would be the interpreter of the very lines he was then writing.[2] Paul saw himself as the authentic guardian of the divine revelation, and the Lord would confirm his words.

Paul was often abrupt in his change of direction; so it was here: his thought moved like lightning to the person of Christ: "Remember Jesus Christ, risen from the dead, of the seed of David, according to my gospel" (2:8). It is remarkable to hear a call like this, uttered with such solemnity; Timothy was to *remember.* He knew the facts of Christ's death and resurrection; but he was also to keep them in mind, under constant review, and in undying remembrance. He was to fix his thoughts on the person of Christ as risen from the dead. The Greek perfect participle implies more than the fact that His resurrection took place in a certain garden at a certain moment of time. It means that He who was raised from the dead is now alive for evermore; death no more has dominion over Him. The phrase combines two strands of truth in such a way as to present something whole and complete. Christ did suffer and die; He was among the dead. But He that was dead rose after the power of an indissoluble life. This fact is then coupled somewhat surprisingly with the fact that He was of the seed of David. Christ not only belonged to the royal house; He could trace His descent in a direct line from the king. There was only one verse elsewhere in which Paul spoke of Christ as "born of the seed of David" (Rom. 1:3); that verse also was linked with His resurrection (Rom. 1:4). The fact of His Davidic lineage after the flesh proved that He was the Son of man; the fact of His resurrection from the dead through the power of the Spirit proved Him to be the Son of God. These two great verities were at the heart of Paul's teaching. He had made use of this phrase *according to my*

2. Moule, *Studies in Second Timothy,* p. 79.

gospel twice before for the sake of impressive emphasis (Rom. 2:16; 16:25). The Incarnation and Resurrection were the keystones of the message which Paul proclaimed as "my gospel."

But the very mention of the gospel, as so often, sent his thoughts off on a tangent, because it was for this cause that Paul found himself in bonds: "wherein I suffer hardship unto bonds, as a malefactor; but the word of God is not bound" (2:9). The word *wherein* makes it clear that it was the cause of the gospel which was at stake in his imprisonment. He had exhorted Timothy to be ready to suffer hardship (2:3); it was Paul's own bitter experience. He had often been in prison as a result of his proclamation of the gospel: in Philippi; perhaps in Ephesus; in Jerusalem; in Caesarea; in Rome. The circumstances varied and the hardship was not always severe. But there was no room for comfort in his present experience; he was in bonds. There were chains on his wrists; perhaps he was handcuffed to a Roman soldier. He was deprived of his freedom even in the space of that cell; he was never allowed to be alone. He was under guard night and day, and was treated as a malefactor. This word occurs in only one other New Testament context, and that was to describe the two criminals who were crucified on each side of the Lord Jesus (Luke 23:32, 39). Perhaps Paul chose that word because it would suggest that he was now treading in his Master's footsteps; he was being treated as a malefactor and numbered with transgressors. It may also furnish a hint as to the charge on which he would be tried: he was wearing chains as if he were a common felon, perhaps because of the disturbances that so often centered round his preaching.[3] But while Paul was in chains, *"the word of God is not bound."* This may refer to the fact that though he was in prison, he could still bear witness to Christ (4:16–17); but it is more likely to have meant

3. Guthrie, *Pastoral Epistles*, p. 143.

that though he was restrained, others were still free to proclaim the Word (Phil. 1:14).

Paul went on to affirm that such hardship was as vital an element as his preaching for the salvation of God's elect: "Therefore I endure all things for the elect's sake, that they also may obtain the salvation which is in Christ Jesus with eternal glory" (2:10). There was no break in the movement of thought; this is made clear by his use of the word *therefore*. It was for this reason that Paul endured hardship whether in the form of bonds and imprisonment or of death itself. He would endure all things as part of that fellowship with Christ in His sufferings which was for the sake of all God's elect. Paul wrote about the same thing in moving language to the Colossians: "I rejoice in my sufferings for your sake, and fill up on my part that which is lacking of the afflictions of Christ in my flesh for his body's sake, which is the church" (Col. 1:24). He spoke of God's elect because he had in view all whom God has chosen. There were some who had yet to come to the point of believing surrender. They would be saved through the preaching of the gospel, but he could not preach the gospel unless he were also to suffer for it. Therefore what he endured was for the purpose "that they also may obtain . . . salvation." Paul both preached and endured for that one great purpose: that they might be saved through Christ forever. H. C. G. Moule made the delightful suggestion that Paul longed to help them "on their way through grace to glory, through Christ on earth to Christ in heaven."[4] That salvation was in Christ Jesus; that is, it was centered in Him alone, and was for all whom faith had drawn into union with Him. It was also with a view to eternal glory; that is, glory was the consummation in view for God's elect. "God chose you from the beginning unto salvation . . . whereunto he called you through our gospel, to the obtaining of the glory of our Lord Jesus Christ" (II Thess. 2:13–14).

4. Moule, *Studies in Second Timothy,* p. 83.

Paul then quoted the last of five faithful sayings which are preserved in these pastoral epistles: "Faithful is the saying: For if we died with him, we shall also live with him: if we endure, we shall also reign with him" (2:11–12). H. C. G. Moule suggests that Paul did not compose these lines, but that he chose to quote "a primeval Christian hymn."[5] This may be only a fragment, but its rhythm and cadence would easily establish it in the minds and hearts of the earliest believers. It soon came to be thought of as a faithful saying on which early Christians could firmly rely. The hymn has two couplets which are proverbial in form and in content. The first couplet concerns those who remain true and endure; the next couplet concerns those who become false and faithless. The first word *for* must look back to words that precede and may refer to part of the hymn which was not quoted. But it may just as well be linked with what Paul wrote about the duty to suffer hardship; to die with Christ was in line with what it meant to endure all things for Him. Paul had used a similar expression before: "if we died with Christ, we believe that we shall also live with him" (Rom. 6:8). It must also recall his even more famous saying: "I have been crucified with Christ; yet I live; and yet no longer I, but Christ liveth in me" (Gal. 2:20). Paul was identified with Christ in such totality that he shared both in His death and in His resurrection. I died with Him; He lives in me: he died daily (I Cor. 15:31); therefore daily he had to bear in his body "the dying of Jesus" (II Cor. 4:10). That meant that there was a never-ceasing call to endure; to endure with patience to the end, but buoyed up with the promise that all those who endure with Christ are also destined to reign with Him.

The next couplet preserves the same rhythmical qualities and is rounded off by one short sentence which corresponds with the introduction about the faithful saying: "if we shall deny him, he also will deny us: if we are faithless, he abideth

5. Ibid., pp. 84–85.

faithful: for he cannot deny himself" (2:12–13). Did Paul have in mind all those in Asia who had turned away from him? There was a throb of pain in Paul's words, for he knew only too well that they described potential attitudes which the lapse of time would reveal. The first line in this new couplet is a direct echo of the solemn warning voiced by the Lord Jesus: "whosoever shall deny me before men, him will I also deny before my Father which is in heaven" (Matt. 10:33). What does it mean to deny Christ? It is to treat Him as Simon Peter did when "he denied, saying, . . . I know him not" (Luke 22:57). Peter *turned away* from Christ (II Tim. 1:15); He swore with oath and curse; he disowned and denied the Lord three times over. Peter was to find his way back along the stern, hard road of true repentance, and he lived to confess the Lord with great courage on numerous occasions. But God does not forgive in the case of final apostasy; instead He will deny those by whom He has been denied. This is the force of that terrible utterance about the workers of iniquity: "then will I profess unto them, I never knew you" (Matt. 7:23). But that dreadful sentence is more dreadful still in light of the next words; they might be faithless, but He is always faithful. Those who deny Christ are faithless; He must deny them just because He is faithful. It is impossible to admit any self-contradiction in God;[6] that is why He cannot deny Himself. The whole of this faithful saying rests on the fact that God cannot deny His own essential character. He must forever be true to Himself; therefore He will be true to us as well.

6. Guthrie, *Pastoral Epistles*, p. 146.

17

*"But thou didst follow my teaching,
conduct, purpose, faith, longsuffering, love,
patience, persecutions, sufferings; what
things befell me at Antioch, at Iconium, at
Lystra; what persecutions I endured: and
out of them all the Lord delivered me."*

II Timothy 3:10-13

Paul now turned his thoughts toward the church and
the surrounding society. "But know this," he wrote, "that in
the last days grievous times shall come" (3:1). The dawn of
the last days had come with the new age of the gospel (Acts
2:16-17; Heb. 1:1-2); it was an age in which formidable seasons,
times of peril and stress, would come.[1] Paul had long been
concerned about the social trends in the Roman Empire. He
had warned the elders of the church in Ephesus in terms
which showed that he foresaw grievous troubles within the
church (Acts 20:29-30), and now he was warning Timothy
who was a resident in Ephesus that these things were at
hand. This led Paul to draw a picture of the men of evil who
would abound in those times of trouble (3:2-5). The list does
not possess any special order but it is not unlike the terrible
catalogue of pagan vices which Paul compiled in his letter to
the Romans. There are nineteen blistering expressions within
the space of three verses which describe the men who were

1. Moule, *Studies in Second Timothy,* p. 107.

responsible for those grievous seasons.[2] Paul began by saying that such men are "lovers of self" (3:2); he ended by saying that they were not "lovers of God" (3:4). All the lurid words in between depict society in a state of appalling decadence. From lovers of money to lovers of pleasure, from those who were boastful and haughty to those who were headstrong and puffed up, the men who are described stand out as men from whose lives the love of God had vanished. The worst feature was that such men might have a form of godliness, but they "denied the power thereof" (3:5). Outward forms of worship might be observed, but the inner reality had gone. From such men, wrote Paul, let Timothy turn away.

Paul then pursued this theme in more detail and began to describe certain types of religious professors who sought their own self-interest under the cloak of an insidious propaganda: "For of these are they that creep into houses, and take captive silly women" (3:6). They wormed their way into homes where women were an easy prey for plausible visitors. The term *silly women* would be better rendered little women, and it was a term of contempt for those who were weak and idle. There was moral weakness: the Ephesians were "laden with sins, led away by divers lusts" (3:6). Their conscience was restless; their sin was a burden too great to bear; they were haunted by fear. There was also mental weakness: they were "ever learning, and never able to come to the knowledge of the truth" (3:7). They were unstable in mind; they were credulous in faith; they were gullible in what concerned the truth. They were weak in character and in intellect,[3] and were taken captive by the predatory propagandists of a spurious religion. Paul then likened such men to the legendary figures of Jannes and Jambres who were believed to have been the men who withstood Moses in the court of Pharaoh (see Exod. 7:11): these men in like manner withstood

2. Stott, *Guard the Gospel*, p. 84.
3. Ibid., p. 89.

the truth, and denied the faith (3:8). But the comparison went much further, for its tacit implication was that Paul had likened himself to God's servant Moses. Indeed all that Moses had been under the law, Paul had become in the new age of the gospel. The wickedness and blasphemy of those religious charlatans would be just as short-lived as that of the Egyptian sorcerers: "they shall proceed no further: for their folly shall be evident unto all men, as theirs also came to be" (3:9).

Timothy's attitude was far removed from that of those evil-minded teachers, and the emphatic personal pronoun *thou* points up the contrast: "But thou didst follow my teaching, conduct, purpose, faith, longsuffering, love, patience" (3:10). There were many who had misused the truth or turned away from the faith, but as for Timothy, he had diligently observed the whole range of life and doctrine exemplified by Paul. It is very striking at times to see how Paul dared to appeal to his own life, his teaching and conduct, as the standard for his converts to keep in mind. "Be ye imitators of me," he had written, "even as I also am of Christ (I Cor. 11:1; cf. I Thess. 1:6; Phil. 3:17). Timothy had followed Paul's example in this spirit; he had been a pupil who had modeled himself on the pattern of his teacher with the dedicated perseverance of a totally committed disciple. Paul then listed seven distinct items which summed up his doctrine, manner of life, motives and general demeanor. He began with teaching; this was crucial at a time of frenzied debate and false philosophy. But his doctrine did not stand by itself; it was intimately linked with the kind of life he lived. The test of truth would be seen in conduct; and in Paul's case, his way of life was well known to all those who came into contact with him. It was confirmed by his sense of purpose; for his aim in life was the key to his motives. The four virtues, faith, longsuffering, love, patience, were all derived from Christ Himself, and may be set out in paraphrastic form as faithfulness, tolerance, charity, endurance. Three of them had already been enjoined on Timothy: "But

thou, O man of God, . . . follow after . . . faith, love, patience"
(I Tim. 6:11). Paul's claim in this verse was that his own life
furnished an example of all that he enjoined on Timothy.

Paul then moved from the marks of personal character to
a touching fragment of autobiography: "persecutions, sufferings; what things befell me at Antioch, at Iconium, at Lystra;
what persecutions I endured: and out of them all the Lord
delivered me" (3:11). The quality of endurance just mentioned
might well prompt this recollection of persecutions and sufferings. It might have been enough to list the fact and then
pass on; but Paul chose to be more explicit. He might have
dwelt on the imprisonment and bonds which he had to
endure at that very moment; he had done so before. But he
went back to the things that befell him in the three upland
cities he visited while on his first missionary journey. What
he wrote was very simple, full of human pathos, evoking
memories still vivid and poignant. It may have been as a
result of the persecution Paul suffered on that journey that
his leadership was established. He would remember Antioch
where the Jews had stirred up so much opposition that he
and Barnabas were driven out of the city (Acts 13:50). He
would recall Iconium where the Jews had conspired with the
gentiles "to entreat them shamefully and to stone them" (Acts
14:5). He would never forget Lystra where Jews from Antioch
and Iconium had prevailed on the ignorant multitude to stone
him, to drag him out of the city, and to leave him for dead
(Acts 14:19). Nothing could erase that terrible experience from
Paul's memory: "I bear branded on my body the marks of
Jesus" (Gal. 6:17). Timothy would remember, too. He would
have heard all that happened in Antioch and Iconium; he
may have seen what took place in Lystra. He knew well *what
persecutions* Paul had endured; he knew as well how the
Lord had rescued Paul from them all.

Paul's own bitter experience was an illustration of the hostility which would in some measure await all who identified
themselves with the Lord Jesus: "Yea, and all that would live

godly in Christ Jesus shall suffer persecution" (3:12). The word *yea* marks the swing away from Paul's own trials to those which would beset all who followed in the footprints of Christ. The word *all* is emphatic by its position in the Greek text, but the underlying thought was specially directed toward Timothy. Paul and Barnabas had left Lystra and gone on to Derbe. Then they could have followed the road down to Tarsus where they would have found friends. Instead with great courage they had retraced their steps and had paid a return visit to the cities from which they had been driven out. There was no fresh act of persecution, perhaps because they confined themselves to their converts. Paul and Barnabas confirmed and strengthened the faith of the new Christians, exhorted them to persevere, and warned them "that through many tribulations we must enter into the kingdom of God" (Acts 14:22). Those new gentile converts had witnessed the persecution Paul had endured; it was through such persecution that they also would come into the joy of God's kingdom. Perhaps that brave exhortation had been revived in his mind as he now wrote of those three cities. His words of long ago were as real and relevant for Timothy in Ephesus as when they had first been uttered. They were applied to all that would live godly by virtue of union with Christ Jesus. The new converts were called to lead a godly life in the midst of a godless society; and the contradiction between godliness and godlessness would always provoke opposition. It would be as the Lord Himself foretold; they would suffer persecution. This was a fact of life for the earliest Christians; they knew that there was no easy way out. And in some form, persecution, tribulation, opposition, must touch the lives of all, in all generations and all societies, who seek to live godly in Christ Jesus.

The text abruptly reverts back to the main theme in the opening paragraph of this chapter: "But evil men and impostors shall wax worse and worse, deceiving and being deceived" (3:13). Persecution of the godly would prove inevitable because of the "progressive worsening" of a situation in which evil-minded men and religious impostors prevailed.[4] Paul was so provoked by those whose aim was to exploit the truth for gain that no words were too strong for him to use. He denounced Elymas the sorcerer in horrifying language: "full of all guile and all villany, thou son of the devil, thou enemy of all righteousness" (Acts 13:10). Paul had been "sore troubled" by the slave girl who was possessed with a spirit of divination (Acts 16:18). He had seen the discomfiture of the seven sons of Sceva who fled "naked and wounded" (Acts 19:16). Now he spoke of impostors, sorcerers, charlatans, thinking of the Egyptian sorcerers who had withstood Moses (see 3:8). They would wax worse and worse. The verb means to go on, to make progress; and he used it with an obvious irony. They would progress only from what was bad to what was worse. The same verb had been used of them before: "They shall proceed no further" (3:9). There were indeed limits to the extent of their success as false teachers; but there were no limits to the moral deterioration in their own minds. Such men tried to operate as deceivers, but in the end they would themselves be deceived (see Titus 3:3). They would come to believe their own falsehoods, and what they had done to others would happen to them. The practice of deceit results in self-deceit and their last state would be worse than their first. A tense statement, a grim judgment, and a sobering prophecy.

4. Guthrie, *Pastoral Epistles*, p. 161.

18

"But abide thou in the things which thou hast learned and hast been assured of, knowing of whom thou hast learned them."

II Timothy 3:14-17

Paul turned away from his warnings about evil men and impostors to address himself once more in a strongly personal vein to Timothy: "But abide thou in the things which thou hast learned and hast been assured of, knowing of whom thou hast learned them" (3:14). Evil-minded men would go from bad to worse; it was like a disease which could progress only toward one end. But as for Timothy, he was to abide, and so continue (AV) in what he had learned and believed. The word *abide* meant to remain, to stand fast where he was. He was to "cultivate stability"[1] so that he would not be shaken by novelty or heresy. Timothy was to stand by the things he had learned and of which he had been assured. These things were the doctrines of grace in which he had been trained over the years. He had learned them, and had become assured of them; he had been taught the truth and had come to a strong personal conviction that it was true indeed. Further, he was strengthened in what he had come to believe when he recalled by whom it had been taught. The word Paul used was indefinite; it meant persons, but did not speak of them by name. But the context suggests that Paul would have Timothy look back to his childhood, the

1. Stott, *Guard the Gospel,* p. 98.

home where Lois and Eunice had brought him up in the fear and nurture of the Lord (see 1:5). But it would be wrong to limit the word in its application; it would also refer to Paul himself. Paul had constantly reminded Timothy of his teaching: "Hold the pattern of sound words which thou hast heard from me" (1:13); "the things which thou hast heard from me among many witnesses . . ." (2:2). Paul had been his mentor in all these things. Timothy had to continue in what he had been taught.

Paul pressed this point with a cogent appeal to the experience of Timothy's childhood: "and that from a babe thou hast known the sacred writings which are able to make thee wise unto salvation through faith which is in Christ Jesus" (3:15). The phrase "from a babe" must imply that the faith which dwelt both in Timothy's mother and grandmother had been of long standing, for he had been nurtured in the pure milk of the word right from the cradle. This must further imply that long before Lois and Eunice had come to a saving trust in the Lord Jesus they had both been devoted adherents of the faith and vision of their fathers. So from childhood, Timothy had known the sacred writings; an unusual, perhaps a technical term for Holy Scripture. In this context it would mark its special value as against the dubious elements in the literature of the pseudo-teachers. It was a term which could refer only to the canonical books of the Old Testament: the Law, the Psalms, and the Prophets. What was written was able to make him wise with a view to salvation. This is comparable with a statement by James to the effect that "the implanted word . . . is able to save your souls" (James 1:21). Paul had also reminded the elders of Ephesus of "the word of his grace, which is able to build you up and to give you the inheritance among all them that are sanctified" (Acts 20:32). Accordingly Timothy was reminded that Holy Scripture was able to instruct him with one great end in view: salvation through faith which is in Christ Jesus. So Timothy was saved through faith, and this was "the salvation which is in Christ

Jesus with eternal glory" (2:10). The promise of life, the purpose of grace, faith and love, grace itself: all, like eternal salvation, were to be found only in Christ Jesus (1:1, 9, 13; 2:1).

But one may dwell longer on the underlying significance of Paul's brief words: "From a babe thou hast known the sacred writings." The Old Testament is the foundation of the Bible as a revelation of the character of God and His purposes for man. This was of primary importance in the national history of the tribes of Israel. Moses gave his people the law, and the prophets taught them that God alone is God. That was why Paul posed a rhetorical question to which he supplied the answer: "What advantage then hath the Jew? or what is the profit of circumcision?" (Rom. 3:1); that is, what advantage does the Jew enjoy in comparison with the Gentiles? Paul was quick to reply: "Much every way: first of all, that they were intrusted with the oracles of God" (Rom. 3:2). This meant little or nothing in the ancient world of pagan culture. The best of the gentiles, men such as Socrates or Scipio, knew no more of truth than they could learn from the variable light of nature and reason. But the Jews were the appointed guardians of God's great self-revelation in the Scriptures, and their national history had turned and would turn on the hinge of their conduct as its trustees. The kingdom of Israel prospered under rulers who worshiped God, and honored the law, and obeyed its precepts. It began to decline and plunged into headlong ruin when it ignored God's word and will. The history of Judaism for two thousand years since Paul's day has borne witness to the reality of this pattern. The Jews lost their identity as a nation while they kept their identity as a people. It is only in this generation that the world has seen their rehabilitation as a national entity in the modern Israel. But will Israel today hearken to God's word and become wise unto salvation?

Paul would not let go of this theme; he had more of great significance to say: "Every Scripture inspired of God is also profitable for teaching, for reproof, for correction, for instruction which is in righteousness" (3:16). There is no doubt that the Revised Version tends to obscure one main aspect of Paul's meaning; this is because of its failure to make adequate allowance for one small word: *also.* Paul wanted to assert two facts about Scripture, and the real force of his sentence is lost unless it is broken into two parts: "Every Scripture [is] inspired of God [and] is also profitable for teaching. . . ." It was the fact of its divine inspiration that rendered it profitable. The phrase "inspired of God" translates a single compound word in the Greek text. The most literal translation is often used: God-breathed. But that is an awkward word in English and it is more euphonious to read breathed of God. H. C. G. Moule said that "the breath of God was in each Scripture as man's breath is in his words."[2] This is in harmony with the Petrine saying: "the prophecy came not in old time by the will of man: but holy men of God spake as they were moved by the Holy Ghost" (II Peter 1:21, AV). So Paul himself had dared to claim that he spoke ". . . not in words which man's wisdom teacheth, but which the Spirit teacheth" (I Cor. 2:13). The mind of God was made known through the word of God; God breathed it; God spoke it; it was inspired of God. And Scripture so inspired is of everlasting value as a guide or rule for doctrine and for conduct. As for doctrine, it is profitable both for imparting the truth and for rebuking error; as for conduct, it is profitable both for reformation of bad manners and for training in the right way of life.

But once more one may dwell on the underlying significance of Paul's brief words: "All Scripture is given by inspiration of God" (3:16, AV). God's self-revelation through the sacred writings would have had no value unless it were accompanied by the inspiration of the written record. It would have left men in doubt and uncertainty. That great fact of divine revelation was so truly unique that one may

2. Moule, *Studies in Second Timothy,* p. 123.

say, very reverently, that God perforce had to add the fact of divine inspiration. When Paul spoke of inspiration, he did not mean that the Scriptures are merely a noble piece of literature in the sense that is meant when men speak of the works of Homer or Virgil as having been inspired. Neither did Paul hold some fanciful theory of mechanical dictation or automatic utterance, as though men fell into a trance and wrote what they were moved to write without conscious control. What Paul meant was that God so possessed the heart and mind of each human writer that His thoughts were as their thoughts and that His words were as their words. It was only to the original text that inspiration in this manner could be rightly applied, but that inspiration was the guarantee of its character as a record of the divine revelation. It was perfectly obvious that the human authors did not follow the same literary patterns; there were always personal elements discernible in speech and style. But that did not alter God's plan; He used all the authors as vehicles or instruments in order to convey the truth. Behind every human writer in each successive century was the Spirit of God breathing through them the word of God.

The whole section concludes with a statement of the purpose for which Scripture was given: "that the man of God may be complete, furnished completely unto every good work" (3:17). Who was "the man of God" Paul had in mind? Was it no more than a general reference which could have been applied at will? Perhaps so; but Paul exhorted Timothy on an earlier occasion with this striking designation: "But thou, O man of God, flee these things" (I Tim. 6:11). Further, this section began with an emphatic personal address: "But abide thou in the things which thou hast learned and hast been assured of" (3:14). Therefore it seems reasonable to treat "the man of God" in this context as an indirect reference to Timothy. Holy Scripture was of untold value for such a man because it could build him up in spiritual stature until he was complete in Christ. The word *complete* means "perfect"

(AV) or mature; to be complete was a mark of spiritual maturity. Donald Guthrie observes that it "describes a man perfectly adapted for his task."[3] Another phrase amplifies the effect of this statement and by its use of a cognate verb clothes it with impressive emphasis. This is made clear in the literal translation of the Revised Version: "furnished completely unto every good work." One may prefer the more musical translation of the Authorized Version: "throughly furnished unto all good works." It is akin to an earlier utterance: "he shall be a vessel unto honour, sanctified, meet for the master's use, prepared unto every good work" (2:21). The Word of God must be the one *"vade-mecum"*[4] for all who would bear the name of a man of God; by it that man may be throughly furnished, fully equipped for all God has for him to do.

3. Guthrie, *Pastoral Epistles*, p. 165.
4. Simpson, *Pastoral Epistles*, p. 151.

"Henceforth there is laid up for me the crown of righteousness, which the Lord, the righteous judge, shall give to me at that day: and not only to me, but also to all them that have loved his appearing."

II Timothy 4:1–8

We now listen to the farewell message of the veteran apostle as this letter moves to a close with its mingled "chords of threnody and triumph":[1] "I charge thee in the sight of God, and of Christ Jesus, who shall judge the quick and the dead, and by his appearing and his kingdom; preach the word; be instant in season, out of season; reprove, rebuke, exhort, with all longsuffering and teaching" (4:1–2). The authority and solemnity of this address would be heightened by Paul's sense of the majesty and holiness of God. Paul's first letter contained a charge which began in terms that were almost identical, though it had a different objective: "I charge thee in the sight of God, and Christ Jesus, and the elect angels, that thou observe these things . . ." (I Tim. 5:21). In place of "the elect angels," there is here an extended reference to the office of Christ as Judge of the quick and the dead. Perhaps the near approach of death brought the prospect of that final judgment into immediate focus. But Paul went on to add the phrase "by his appearing and his kingdom." Paul wrote of Christ's return as an event which

1. Simpson, *Pastoral Epistles*, p. 151.

would herald the last judgment and the consummation of His kingdom. It was in the light of all this that Paul adjured Timothy to fulfil his ministry. The five verbs that followed were all in the aorist tense which seems to suggest that Timothy was in a crisis situation. First and foremost, he was to preach the word; that is, "the sound doctrine" (4:3) of the sacred writings which had nourished him from childhood. He had heard it and believed it; he had been called to guard it and suffer for it; he must also preach it. That meant that he must be instant in season, out of season; he must always be on duty, whether the moment were convenient for him or not. The summons to reprove, rebuke, exhort, describes certain aspects of such urgent preaching. If those words hint at severity, they are softened by the demand that they should be accompanied by patient understanding and sound doctrine.

The element of urgency is then elucidated by Paul's warning of the coming hostility to the gospel in all quarters: "For the time will come when they will not endure the sound doctrine; but, having itching ears, will heap to themselves teachers after their own lusts; and will turn away their ears from the truth, and turn aside unto fables" (4:3-4). Paul might have been mindful of his imprisonment and bonds, and that might have led him to speak of political adversity and growing persecution. But his thoughts were centered on the opposition that would arise when men could not endure the truth and chose fables instead. It is clear that such an attitude was even then prevalent, and it was not hard to foresee that the time was at hand when things would be still less favorable. Paul had foretold that "in the last days grievous times shall come" (3:1). One mark of those days would be that men would no longer endure the sound doctrine (see I Tim. 1:10); they would not listen to the truth; they would refuse to hear. Their craving for something else would be like an itch which they could not control. To have itching ears meant that their hearing could be tickled, "as if what they heard merely scratched their eardrums without penetrating further."[2] Therefore they would amass teachers who would be to their own liking and would pander to their caprice. Worse yet, men who lacked all serious intention would not only refuse the truth, but would also succumb to the lure of fanciful counterfeits. They would wander in the by-paths of myth (I Tim. 1:4, 6); they would go in pursuit of fables. This would be the sign of ultimate defection; namely, the choice of myth rather than truth.

But in contrast with the spiritual decline of those dark days, a fresh summons for diligence and devotion in the exercise of Timothy's ministry rang out: "But be thou sober in all things, suffer hardship, do the work of an evangelist, fulfil thy ministry" (4:5). Once more, the pronoun *thou* is emphatic: *but as for you* (see 3:10, 14). Timothy's attention was called to four imperatives which were framed in full view of his current situation. He was to be sober, sober-minded, in all things; he was to school himself so that he would remain cool and sane and watchful in the midst of chaos. This was to be his stance in marked contrast with that of the unstable multitude. Then he was to suffer hardship; Timothy would indeed need that presence of mind as he encountered various forms of trouble. Paul had made it plain that Timothy was called to endure hardship for the gospel (1:8), and to share such hardship with him (2:3). There could be no escape from the offense of the cross; the preaching of the cross would always provoke the scorn of the gentiles. Nevertheless Timothy was to do the work of an evangelist; a word only used twice elsewhere. It had described Philip and his work in Samaria (Acts 21:8); and it appeared in the list of workmen whom God gave to the church (Eph. 4:11). It stood "midway between apostles and prophets on the one hand, and pastors and teachers on the other."[3] Paul clearly wanted Timothy to make the proclamation of the gospel the central

2. Guthrie, *Pastoral Epistles*, p. 167.
3. Ibid., p. 168.

and crucial feature of his life's work. The last summons was the proper sequel: "fulfil thy ministry." It was like the call to Archippus: "Take heed to the ministry which thou hast received in the Lord, that thou fulfil it" (Col. 4:17). Timothy was to "persevere until his task (was) accomplished."[4]

The strong clarion call to Timothy was made in the knowledge that Paul's life of dedicated service was now almost over, and the contrast between the two emphatic personal pronouns, *but thou ... for I,* marks the sequence of thought: "For I am already being offered, and the time of my departure is come" (4:6). These words form the introduction to one of Paul's final and most moving declarations; it is impossible, even at this distance in time, to read his words and not to feel deeply aroused. A succession of metaphors runs through the whole passage; two of them spring from the verbs in this verse. The first picturesque metaphor was drawn from the altar: he was already being offered. Paul employed the same figure of speech in a former imprisonment: "Yea, and if I am offered upon the sacrifice and service of your faith, I joy, and rejoice with you all" (Phil. 2:17). The word had a sacrificial content; it meant to be poured out as a libation or drink-offering. Paul knew that his death would come by the sword, and his lifeblood would be poured out as that of a martyr. It would be an offering, or a libation, for the glory of God. The next metaphor was a complement to this idea; it spoke of the time of departure as now imminent. Paul had also used this figure of speech in that former imprisonment: "having the desire to depart and be with Christ" (Phil. 1:23). Paul was like a soldier, ready to strike his tent and fall into line for the march of a new day. He was like a vessel, ready to weigh anchor, slip its moorings, and sail for a new shore. Death would loose him and set him free from all the ties of earth and time, and he could look forward with an unruffled countenance to that moment when he would be with Christ; for that would be far, far better (Phil. 1:23).

4. Stott, *Guard the Gospel,* p. 112.

That led Paul to pause in deliberate recollection of all that was now past, and three laconic expressions in the form of old and favorite metaphors follow: "I have fought the good fight, I have finished the course, I have kept the faith" (4:7). Each verb in the perfect tense had the ring of finality because the end was in sight, and the pictures that flashed across Paul's mind summed up the whole thrust of his life. His first picture was that of a soldier: he had fought the good fight. The verb could have referred to a contest such as wrestling; but there was a soldier on guard and what was more likely than the image of a warfare which was now accomplished (cf. I Tim. 1:18)? It was just what Paul had enjoined on his younger partner: "Fight the good fight of the faith" (I Tim. 6:12). And Paul had now done it; he had fought to the end; the battle was over. The next picture was that of an athlete: he had finished the course. He had pictured himself as a man with one aim: he pressed toward the mark for the prize of God's high calling which is in Christ Jesus (Phil. 3:14). Paul's own aspirations had been summed up in a memorable statement to the elders of Ephesus. Bonds and imprisonment might be in store for him: "But none of these things move me, neither count I my life dear unto myself, so that I might finish my course with joy" (Acts 20:24, AV). And Paul had now done it; he had stayed on the course; he had reached the goal. The third picture was that of a trustee: he had kept the faith. This was in line with Paul's repeated reference to the need to guard the deposit which was committed into their care (I Tim. 1:11; II Tim. 1:12). And Paul had now done it; his trust had been fulfilled; the faith he held was intact. What a review! The fight for the soldier, the race for the athlete; the task for the trustee: now it was all like a finished story.

Therefore Paul could turn from the past and the present to the future and could rejoice at the prospect of the victor's wreath or garland which he would then receive at the hands of that Judge who cannot err: "henceforth there is laid up for me the crown of righteousness, which the Lord, the righteous judge, shall give to me at that day: and not only to me, but also to all them that have loved his appearing" (4:8). Paul's thinking was colored by a fresh and glorious metaphor as he drew to a close. The word *henceforth* marks the contrast between what was finished and what was still to come; it was itself the sign of the forward-looking vision of faith. He spoke of what had been laid up for him, just as he had spoken of "the hope which is laid up for you in the heavens" (Col. 1:5). There was in store for him the crown of righteousness (cf. James 1:12; Rev. 2:10). The crown was the wreath of honor placed on the brow of the winning athlete in the Greek games; it was highly prized, but perishable. Paul, however, had more in mind than an athlete's garland; it was the crown, not of victory, but of righteousness; that is, the grand vindication which the Lord would grant Paul on the day of judgment. One can hardly doubt the implied contrast between the Lord who is the righteous Judge and Nero who was notorious for his unjust verdicts. Nero might pronounce Paul guilty and sentence him to death; but the Lord would acquit Paul in that day when He will judge the world in righteousness and in truth. Nor would Paul be unique in that experience; it will await "all who have set their love on His appearing";[5] so Moule tried to capture the thought behind the Greek perfect participle. They look for the coming glory of the risen Savior, for at that day He will receive them as righteous in the presence of God for time and for eternity.

5. Moule, *Studies in Second Timothy*, p. 149.

"The Lord will deliver me from every evil work, and will save me unto his heavenly kingdom: to whom be the glory forever and ever. Amen."

II Timothy 4:9-18

These words were among the last that Paul would ever write, therefore they have a far more moving appeal than would otherwise have been the case. Overtones of loneliness, heartache, pathos, tenderness are evident. Paul's first and last instructions were for Timothy alone. "Do thy diligence to come shortly unto me. . . . Do thy diligence to come before winter" (4:9, 21). If they were to meet once more, there was no time to lose: he must come soon, while Paul was yet alive; and he must come before winter, when the sea lanes were closed. Paul longed night and day to see him (1:3–4), and that longing would be increased by the absence of three trusted colleagues. Crescens had gone to Galatia, that is, in all likelihood, to Gaul; Titus had gone to Dalmatia, probably on the Adriatic coastline; Tychicus had gone or was going to Ephesus, perhaps as the bearer of this letter. Other friends were scattered round the Levant; Paul missed them all. Carpus, the man who may have been Paul's host on an earlier occasion, was in Troas (see Acts 20:7); Erastus, the man no doubt who had become Timothy's companion on a special journey, was in Corinth (see Acts 19:22); Trophimus, the citizen of Ephesus who had accompanied Paul to Jerusalem, was in Miletus (see Acts 21:29). There is one more sentence very striking in sheer simplicity: "Only Luke is with me" (4:11). So this beloved physician was the only one who stood by Paul with unshaken loyalty when he was most alone. But Paul went on to add: "Take Mark, and bring him with thee: for he is useful to me for ministering" (4:11). This meant that the breach had been healed and Mark was back in the Pauline circle. The names of Crescens and Carpus are new; all the others were names of men whom Paul had known and loved as his fellow-workers.

But there were two who caused Paul great pain and sadness, and the first more than the second: "Demas forsook me, having loved this present world" (4:10). Demas had been coupled with Luke when Paul wrote to the Colossian believers (Col. 4:14), and again with Epaphras, Mark, Aristarchus and Luke in the Epistle to Philemon (Philem. 24). But in painful contrast with Luke, Demas had left Paul in the lurch. Unlike those who had set their hearts on His glorious appearing, Demas had set his heart on the worldly present. Perhaps his one desire was "to be out of the way of the dungeon and the scaffold,"[1] and he had gone off to bury himself in Thessalonica. But Paul saw this as an act of personal desertion and was saddened beyond the skill of words to tell. But the second cause of sorrow was different in character and Paul's response was far more vehement: "Alexander the coppersmith did me much evil: the Lord will render to him according to his works: of whom be thou ware also; for he greatly withstood our words" (4:14–15). Who was Alexander? Was he the orator who was pushed forward by the Jews in the great uproar at Ephesus (Acts 19:23)? Was he the heretic who had made shipwreck of his faith and whom Paul had consigned to Satan (I Tim. 1:20)? It is impossible to say, but Alexander had done great harm to Paul and had strongly opposed Paul's words. Was Alexander the informer who was responsible for Paul's arrest? Was he a witness for the prosecution at Paul's

1. Moule, *Studies in Second Timothy*, p. 151.

first defense? It is clear that Alexander had wronged Paul when Paul was most vulnerable. Alexander seems to have been known to Timothy as well, and Timothy would need to be on his guard. The strength of Paul's feeling is marked by the severity of his verdict about divine retribution for all Alexander's works.

The mention of Alexander would pave the way for some account of the first stage of Paul's defense or trial: "At my first defense no one took my part, but all forsook me: may it not be laid to their account" (4:16). "His first defense" refers to the preliminary investigation that took place before the trial itself. Paul did not state the charge which had been brought against his name; it must have been far more serious than on the last occasion when he had been accused by the Jews from Jerusalem. He was no doubt exposed to the charge of treason as an atheist or an enemy of the imperator. He had become one lone witness in the court of Nero for that other king whose name is Jesus. This was why an adverse verdict would lead to a sentence of death. Paul was probably subject to a barrage of statements and questions; evidence would have been called in order to establish grounds for the trial. He should have been allowed the legal advice or moral support of an advocate who could argue in his defense. But this had been denied: "No one took my part, but all forsook me."[2] This was not a lament for the absence of local friends such as Eubulus and Pudens and Linus and Claudia; still less of Luke. It was simple regret that no qualified advocate would take up Paul's case or speak on his behalf; no one would risk his career, perhaps his safety, in order to defend someone in a trial for treason. Paul understood their position; his heart went out to them; "may it not be laid to their charge." Those words were not only magnanimous; they were

2. "None stood with Paul at the preliminary hearing. Such prominence was perilous. A gust of loneliness can sometimes chill a faithful heart. G. K. Chesterton caught the thought in the poem The Ballad of the White Horse. England's Christian

an echo of the dying voice of Stephen. "Lord," he cried as he fell beneath the storm of stones, "lay not this sin to their charge" (Acts 7:60). Never could Paul forget. So let those who had failed him be gently dealt with at the hands of their Judge.

There was a flash of the old fire in Paul's words as he recalled that scene: "But the Lord stood by me and strengthened me; that through me the message might be fully proclaimed, and that all the Gentiles might hear: and I was delivered out of the mouth of the lion" (4:17). The word *but* has the force of a word like *notwithstanding*, so great was the contrast. When Paul was held in the fortress of Antonia overlooking the temple, "the Lord stood by him, and said, Be of good cheer" (Acts 23:11). When the ship in which Paul traveled under military escort was in extreme danger, he was able to say: "there stood by me this night the angel of God whose I am, and whom I serve, saying, Fear not" (Acts 27:23-24, AV). So now Paul could write of his first ordeal: "The Lord stood by me and strengthened me" (cf. Luke 22:43). Paul was deeply aware that he had not been left to stand alone, Jesus was with him, as He had been with Stephen (Acts 7:56). That strength gave Paul the strong moral

---

king was standing at bay exactly eleven centuries ago. The disastrous battle at Reading had just been fought. A mindless horde of barbarians was breaking like some polluted sea all round his harassed land:

> But Alfred up against them bare,
> And gripped the ground and grasped the air,
> Staggered and strove to stand.
> He bent them back with spear and spade,
> With desperate dyke and wall,
> With foemen leaning on his shield,
> And roaring on him when he reeled,
> And no help came at all. . . .

You catch the note of despair in the last line? As the battle thickens that mood can daunt the heart. It is an illusion, none the less, as Paul said. The Lord was with him." (E. M. Blaiklock, *The Pastoral Epistles, A Study Guide*, pp. 123-24.)

support which he sorely needed that through him the message might be fully proclaimed. He felt that his calling as a preacher was not wholly fulfilled until he had proclaimed God's Word in the imperial city of Rome. But now Paul had discharged that trust in full so that "all the gentiles might hear." It is very moving to find that the gentiles were so deeply engraved on Paul's heart in that hour of trial. He had spoken "as his own counsel in his own defense";[3] but Paul's greatest concern had been that he might bear witness to Christ. That great proclamation had now been made before the most august body in the Roman Empire. What did they make of it? They found that they could not treat Paul as a fanatic, or an impostor, or an anarchist; they could only send him back to prison on remand for formal trial and condemnation. Meanwhile he was delivered out of the mouth of the lion; like Daniel, Paul had been rescued from immediate peril.

So Paul in his unselfconscious style drew one of the great pictures of a man of God on the eve of a violent martyrdom: "The Lord will deliver me from every evil work, and will save me unto his heavenly kingdom: to whom be the glory for ever and ever. Amen" (4:18). There was a swift movement of thought from the phrase "I was delivered" (v. 17) to the phrase "the Lord will deliver." Paul was too much of a realist to hope for his release from that Roman prison. Rather, he had in mind the vast contrast between his recent deliverance from an earthly peril and his preservation for the "everlasting enfranchisement so near at hand."[4] Paul's words are like those of the prayer: "deliver us from the evil one" (Matt. 6:13). Paul had unshaken confidence that the Lord would deliver him from every evil work; no evil could befall him unless God allowed it for his good (see Rom. 8:28). The Lord would not only preserve Paul from evil, but would save him "unto his heavenly kingdom." Nero might send Paul out to die at the

3. Moule, *Studies in Second Timothy,* p. 173.
4. Simpson, *Pastoral Epistles,* p. 161.

point of a sword, but what did that matter? The Lord would keep him safe, would hold him fast, and would bring him into His heavenly kingdom. That phrase stands as unique in Paul's usage though it may well reflect dominical teaching about the kingdom of heaven. Paul used it here to show that all temporal dominion in an earthly empire was as nothing compared with the sovereign majesty of God's everlasting kingdom. And the splendor of that vision made Paul forget all the indignities of the present while he voiced a doxology in the spirit of praise and of worship: "to whom be the glory for ever and ever." It was enough; Paul would add only his solemn Amen; so be it, Lord.

So this study might end; but there is a postscript. H. C. G. Moule was the first to point out that Paul's story had a remarkable sequel.[5] In May 1535, William Tyndale was placed under arrest and thrown into prison in the Castle of Vilvorde. There he was to languish until his trial and execution in August 1536. But one letter, written by his hand in Latin, is still preserved in the archives of the Council of Brabant. It was written during the long winter months of 1535–1536 and addressed to the Marquis of Bergen as Governor of Vilvorde. "I beg your Lordship," he wrote, "and that by the Lord Jesus, that if I am to remain here through the winter, you will request the Commissary to have the kindness to send me from the goods of mine which he has, a warmer cap; for I suffer greatly from cold in the head and am afflicted by a perpetual catarrh which is much increased in this cell; a warmer coat also, for this which I have is very thin; a piece of cloth too to patch my leggings. My overcoat is worn out; my shirts are also worn out. He has a woollen shirt, if he will be good enough to send it. I have also with him leggings of thicker cloth to put on above; he has also warmer night caps. And I ask to be allowed to have a lamp in the evening; it is indeed wearisome, sitting alone in the dark. But most of all I

5. Moule, *Studies in Second Timothy*, pp. 158–59.

beg and beseech your clemency to be urgent with the Commissary that he will kindly permit me to have the Hebrew Bible, Hebrew grammar, and Hebrew dictionary, that I may pass the time in that study. In return, may you obtain what you most desire, so only that it be for the salvation of your soul."[6] Strength and patience meet and mingle in that letter; it breathes the true spirit of dignity and endurance. And the picture of that lonely captive in his threadbare garments, facing ultimate martyrdom, sitting cold and dark and solitary during the long cheerless nights of winter, longing for the solace of light, warm clothes, and books, is like that of Paul as seen through his words: "The cloke that I left at Troas . . . bring when thou comest, and the books, especially the parchments" (4:13).

6. James F. Mozley, *William Tyndale*, p. 334.

Conclusion

Paul was truly great: great as an apologist and theologian; great as a missionary and evangelist; great as a pastor and teacher. His greatness as a theologian is seen in his grasp of the doctrines of grace, in its application to the gentiles, and in his lifelong concern for the defense and confirmation of the gospel. His greatness as a missionary is seen in his journeys by land and sea, in his letters to converts and congregations, and in his care for all the churches. Perhaps it is as a pastor and teacher that he stands before us in these three pastoral epistles. He was very human; he was totally dedicated. We see this in his sense of God's presence and his vision of the unseen, his tenderness and vehemence, his long ordeal of suffering, and the final prospect of martyrdom. "None of these things move me," he boldly declared, "neither count I my life dear unto myself, so that I might finish my course with joy" (Acts 20:24, AV). Did he do it? Did he last the distance? His own words rang out the answer as he told Timothy: "I have finished the course" (II Tim. 4:7).

Do we ask what was Paul's secret? It was the grace of God. Salvation for Paul was in Christ alone, through faith alone, by grace alone. Grace made Paul what by nature he could never have become and enabled him to make the claim: "By the grace of God I am what I am" (I Cor. 15:10). Those words were written not in a boastful spirit; there is no hint of arrogance or presumption in that statement. He wrote with a sense of profound humility, mindful of all that he had been as well as of all that he had become. Saul of Tarsus, the arch-persecutor whose hands had been red with the blood of saints, had now become the bondservant of Christ the Lord.

It was as though Paul were to say: "I am what I am only because He is what He is." It was the grace of God at work in Paul's life that made him a new man in Christ. Nothing else in heaven or earth could have made him the kind of man that God meant him to be. As a result, there were two great priorities in his life. One was communion with God: for him, to live was Christ. And the other was compassion for men: he would become all things to all men if by any means he might win some. That was why his call to preach the gospel was marked by such a strong and single-minded purpose: "For we preach not ourselves, but Christ Jesus as Lord, and ourselves as your servants for Jesus' sake" (II Cor. 4:5).

Had Paul been accused of preaching himself rather than Christ? Was that the force of the word *for*, as though something like that was what men had read into the phrase "our gospel" (II Cor. 4:3)? But Paul had called it *our* only because it was what he and his colleagues sought to proclaim; their sole object was to proclaim the Christ, even Jesus, who is the Lord. Then what did Paul mean by the next words: "and ourselves?" That was not part of his gospel; he did not preach himself, not from any point of view, not even in the meanest capacity. The real force of those words was to indicate his position. Jesus is Lord; therefore, we are no more than bondservants or slaves. That was the sole form of self-reference that was permissible in Paul's preaching. His own office was so humble that it would in no sense detract from the unique glory of Christ the Lord.

This was all in total contrast with the secular attitude which was posited as the mark of the world. The Lord Jesus put His finger on that self-seeking ambition in His warning to the disciples: "The kings of the Gentiles have lordship over them.... But ye shall not be so" (Luke 22:25–26). Christ's own life and work had been the exact antithesis of that worldly practice. He had gone in and out as the divine servant; He had taken on Himself the form of one who was a slave. And those who would follow Him were to share the same spirit: "he that is the greater among you, let him become as the younger; and he that is chief, as he that doth serve" (Luke 22:26). Paul had grasped that lesson; he had often described himself as the servant, or slave, of Christ. But in this case, Paul went even further: "Ourselves your servants." He had told them before how he had made himself servant unto all that he might win them for Christ (I Cor. 9:19, AV). He had vigorously disclaimed lordship over their faith because Paul's one concern was to build up their joy (II Cor. 1:24). Now he described himself as the servant of his converts "for Jesus' sake."

There were mingled strains of pathos and power in the simplicity of that final clinching appeal: "for Jesus' sake." It bears comparison with his later moving address: "We pray you in Christ's stead, be ye reconciled to God" (II Cor. 5:20, AV). Of course Paul did not mean that those he served were his masters; there is but one Master, and all that Paul might do was for His sake. It is very striking to see how the name of Jesus stands here alone. It was the name that spoke of His humanity and humility; the name by which He was known while He was on earth. But after His ascent from the Mount of Olives, that name was almost always linked with such titles as Christ and Lord. It is exceptional to find it by itself in a kind of stark and lonely isolation; that must lend some special significance to its use in that way. So it is in this verse: "And ourselves your servants for Jesus' sake." All that Paul did was done in the spirit of Him who came to serve, and it was done, not for himself, but for His sake. George Whitefield was constrained by that moving appeal to voice his own ardent longing; "Let the name of George Whitefield perish if Christ be glorified!"[1]

1. Loane, *Oxford and the Evangelical Succession*, p. 68.

Paul knew that in himself he was nothing at all. Saul of Tarsus had lived as a Pharisee of the Pharisees, a fanatic in religion, and a stranger to God. Then came that great encounter on the road to Damascus. Saul fell to the ground with his hand on his mouth, and his mouth in the dust. That light! It was brighter than the sun when it shone at its height in the sky. That voice! It was like a clap of thunder in the silence of his own heart. That face! It was the Lord Jesus at the right hand of the eternal majesty of God. All Paul's early dreams and selfish aspirations crashed in ruins and for the first time in his life he asked what the Lord would have him to do. It was from that moment that Paul became as it were a new man in a new world. A new life whose center was in Christ had begun, and that life was to run its course until Paul was led out to Tre Fontane to die at the point of a sword and to enter into the joy of his Master's presence. All that Moses had been as God's servant in Old Testament history, Paul had become as the servant of Christ under the New Testament Evangel. So may we say *ave et vale*, until we meet before the throne of God.